SPEAK WHAT WE FEEL

SPEAK WHAT WE FEEL
(NOT WHAT WE OUGHT TO SAY)

FOUR WHO WROTE
IN BLOOD

FREDERICK BUECHNER

HarperOne
An Imprint of HarperCollins Publishers

HarperOne

HarperCollins books may be purchased for educational, business, or sales promotional use. For information, please e-mail the Special Markets Department at SPsales@ harpercollins.com.

HarperCollins Web site: http://www.harpercollins.com
HarperCollins®, ®, and HarperOne™ are trademarks of
HarperCollins Publishers.

FIRST HARPERCOLLINS PAPERBACK EDITION PUBLISHED IN 2004
Designed by Joseph Rutt

Library of Congress Cataloging-in-Publication Data
Buechner, Frederick
Speak what we feel (not what we ought to say) : reflections on
literature and faith / Fredrick Buechner:—1st ed.
p. cm.
ISBN 978–0–06–251753–1
1. English literature—History and criticism. 2. Christianity and
literature–Great Britain—History. 3. Chesterton, G. K. (Gilbert Keith),
1874–1936. Man who was Thursday. 4. Hopkins, Gerard Manley, 1844–1889—
Criticism and interpretation. 5. Twain, Mark, 1835–1910. Adventures of
Huckleberry Finn. 6. Shakespeare, William, 1564–1616. King Lear.
7. Christianity and literature—United States. 8. Faith in literature.
I. Title.
PR408.C47 B84 2001
820.9'382—dc21   2001016962

HB 01.06.2023

For
my new grandson, George,
and my old friend
Malcolm Goldstein

CONTENTS

INTRODUCTION

It is Red Smith who is reported to have said that it's really very easy to be a writer—all you have to do is sit down at the typewriter and open a vein. Typewriters are few and far between these days, and vein-openers have never grown on trees. Good writers, *serious* writers—by which I mean the writers we remember, the ones who have opened our eyes, maybe even our hearts, to things we might never have known without them—all put much of themselves into their books the way Charles Dickens put his horror at the Poor Law of 1834 into *Oliver Twist*, for instance, or Virginia Woolf her complex feelings about her parents into *To the Lighthouse*, or, less overtly, Flannery O'Connor her religious faith into virtually everything she ever wrote. But opening a vein, I think, points to something beyond that.

Vein-opening writers are putting not just themselves into their books, but themselves at their nakedest and most vulnerable. They are putting their pain and their passion into their books the way Jonathan Swift did in *Gulliver's Travels* and Dostoyevsky in *The Brothers Karamazov*, the way Arthur Miller did in *Death of a Salesman*, and William Maxwell in *They Came Like Swallows*. Not all writers do it all the time—even the blood bank recognizes we have only so much blood to give—and many good writers never do it at all either because for one reason or another they don't choose to or they don't quite know how to; it takes a certain kind of unguard-edness, for one thing, a willingness to run risks, including the risk of making a fool of yourself.

But the four writers these pages are about each did it at least once, and that is the most important single thing they have in common. Shakespeare and Gerard Manley Hopkins are both great writers. Mark Twain is a very good but very uneven writer. G. K. Chesterton, for all his wit and intelligence, is a writer who wrote too much for most of it to be first-rate. But what brings them together here is that in at least one work apiece, it seems to me, each of them wrote in his own blood about the darkness of life as he found it and about how for better or worse he managed some-how to survive it, even to embrace it—Hopkins in the "terrible sonnets" of his final years, Mark Twain in *The Adventures of Huckleberry Finn*, G. K. Chesterton in *The Man Who Was Thursday*, and Shakespeare in *King Lear*. It is at the very end of *King Lear*, in fact, that the Duke of Albany says, "The weight of this sad time we must obey, / Speak what we feel, not what we ought to say," and that seems to me to be precisely what Shakespeare himself did in writing this greatest of all his plays and what in their own entirely different ways the other three did after him.

What I have undertaken to do here is to say something first about what the sad times were for each of them—in the case of Shakespeare precious little is known, but with the other three a good deal—and then to consider how those sad times and the way each came eventually to terms with them are reflected in the mas-terpieces they seem to me to have engendered.

Since I have long since come to believe that all of our stories are at their deepest level the same story, it is my hope that in listening to these four say so powerfully not what they thought they *ought* to say, but what they truly *felt*, we may possibly learn something about how to bear the weight of our own sadness.

PART 1

GERARD MANLEY HOPKINS: THE WATCHER AT THE DOOR

In 1886 Gerard Manley Hopkins met a young Irish poet named Katharine Tynan while she was sitting for her portrait in the Dublin studio of J. B. Yeats, father of the great W. B. "A simple, bright-looking Biddy with glossy very pretty red hair, a farmer's daughter," is the way he described her in a letter to a friend, and she in turn described him as "small and childish-looking, yet like a child-sage, nervous too and very sensitive, with a small ivory pale face."

It is hard to imagine a more incongruous pair—the shy, reclusive little Jesuit who had never published a line and the burgeoning young colleen whose work was being touted everywhere—but they became friends of a sort anyway and saw a fair amount of each other for the two or three years that he had left to live. He sent her some books, they exchanged a few letters, and on at least one occasion, together with a Jesuit colleague who was eccentric and bookish in somewhat the same way he was, Hopkins went even so far as to visit her farmhouse at Clondalkin. As token of the ease of their relationship, somewhere along the line she apparently asked him a question generations of his admirers have been asking themselves ever since. How was it that a man like him with all his interest in art and literature had decided to become of all things a priest? For someone as normally reserved and self-effacing as he was, his answer was startlingly straightforward.

"You wouldn't give only the dull ones to Almighty God," is what he is reported to have told her, and one wonders if perhaps at some other unguarded moment he found it possible to tell her with equal candor about what seems to have been the almost unrelieved desolation of those last few years of his life in Dublin, where his decision to be a priest had landed him.

The double-barreled job he had been assigned there was to teach Latin and Greek literature to undergraduates at the newly founded University College, and at the same time to be a fellow of the Royal University of Ireland, which despite its grandiose name was little more than an examining body whose function was simply to grant degrees to successful candidates from a number of nearby colleges and private schools. On the face of it that would have seemed a congenial enough assignment for a man of Hopkins' interests and abilities, but it turned out to be far otherwise.

First of all, the Dublin of his day was the shabby, impoverished relic of what had once been a beautiful city. Its lovely old Georgian mansions had been converted into overcrowded rooming houses; the streets were swarming with tramps, drunks, and begging children. The river Liffey served as the chief public sewer, so that disease was rampant, and the death rate had risen so high that a lot of country people were afraid to come visit. Nor was the college, where Hopkins lived, in much better condition. The building was full of dry rot, sanitary provisions were primitive, and because it stood on very low ground, the basement stank with filth and vermin. Nor, for Hopkins, was all that the worst of it. Thinking that, come winter, he would be in danger of freezing to death, his mother sent him some warm things to wear, and he responded to the gift in a letter he wrote in comic Irish to his favorite sister, Kate. "Be plased tintimate to me mother Im entirely obleeged to her for her genteel offers," he said. "But as titchin warm clothen tis und-her a misapprehinsion shes labourin. Sure twas not the incliminsee of the saysons I was complainin of at all at all. 'Twas the povertee of books and such like educational convainiences." What he refers to is that when the college was turned over to the Jesuits, the entire library was removed to the diocesan seminary at Clonliffe, and when they appealed to the bishop to return it, their petition was ignored. For Hopkins the absence of books was worse than rats in the cellar.

His job as a professor was to teach Greek and Latin literature to undergraduates, and by all accounts he was never much good at it, that child-sized, ivory-pale man. His voice was "weak but sweet, rather plaintive," as a friend remembered it, his manner was vari-ously described as graceful or effeminate, and he had a long, nar-row face that made his head seem almost too large for his body. In his lectures he tended to go on much too long about the kind of niceties of language and poetic meter that fascinated him as much as they left his students cold, and he also made the fatal mistake of telling them that, as a Royal University fellow, he would himself be the one to make up their examination when the day of reckoning came and for that reason would never lecture on any subject that the examination would cover for fear of giving them an unfair advantage over students from other colleges. That being the case, they not unreasonably concluded, there was no particular point in listening to what he *did* lecture to them about and instead spent a good deal of class time talking and laughing and generally cutting up. They made fun of his Conservative English views and at one point burst into gales of merriment when, God only knows why, he confessed to them that he had never seen a naked woman. On another occasion a colleague is said to have come upon him on his back letting a student drag him around the table by his heels to demonstrate what happened to Hector at Troy—another version has it that it was the student who was being dragged by him—and what they made of that one can only imagine. "I do not object to their being rude to me personally," he wrote to Katharine Tynan, "but I do object to their being rude to their professor and a priest."

Nor did his tribulations end with the classes because in addition to them his Royal University duties involved him in not only making out the examinations but also correcting them. They were given five or six times a year to students from the various participating institutions, and after one particular round he wrote to his friend Robert Bridges that "331 accounts of the First Punic War with trimmings have sweated me down to nearer my lees and usual alluvial low water mudflats, groans, despair, and yearning," and in the year 1887 he reckoned that he had gone through seventeen hundred and ninety-five of them, the average yearly number being somewhere between thirteen and eighteen hundred. It would be almost the stuff of comedy if it had not affected him so tragically. The combined drudgery and what he felt to be the futility of his work led him to the verge of a nervous and physical collapse that he was afraid might well end in madness. In addition to that, the strain on his eyes was so painful that he thought he was going blind despite a doctor's assurance to the contrary, and various other indispositions both real and imaginary continually plagued him as well.

Deeper down still and even harder to bear was his sense of alienation from almost everything and everybody. "To seem the stranger lies my lot, my life / Among strangers" is the way one of his last sonnets begins. His staunchly Anglican family, his father in particular, could never entirely forgive him for his conversion to Roman Catholicism during his undergraduate days at Oxford, and although they continued to exchange letters and visits with him throughout his life, the breach was never really mended. Furthermore, he realized that to his Irish colleagues at the college he, as an Englishman, represented the "enemy," and even though a few of them became his friends, he felt that their relationship was always shadowed. Last but by no means least was his feeling of being estranged from his native land. "England, whose honor O all my heart woos, wife / To my creative thought, would neither hear / Me, were I pleading," the sonnet continues, "plead nor do I." In other words England as represented by the handful of old friends and relations he kept sending his poems to over the years did not "hear" them because to do so required such hard work on their part that it seemed scarcely worth the effort. "Plead nor do I" is a case in point, the syntax as tortured as he felt tortured himself by what he increasingly believed was his hopeless failure to communicate.

As high a hope as any he had, not just as a writer but as a Jesuit priest and man of God, was someday to make his voice heard among other voices trying to win England back to the True Faith, but if the unenthusiastic reaction to his poems of even such an old and devoted friend as his Oxford classmate and fellow poet Robert

Bridges was any indication, he came to think he might as well have saved his breath. The obscure words and fanciful coinages, the convoluted syntax, the elaborate metrical notations were simply too difficult and demanding to appeal to much of anybody. The letter does not survive that Bridges wrote him in 1877 on first reading his great elegy on the drowning of the Franciscan nuns, "The Wreck of the Deutschland," which the Jesuit publication he had submitted it to had already rejected, but the gist of it is all too clear from the letter Hopkins wrote back to him. In it we learn that not only did Bridges find the poem virtually incomprehensible except in bits and pieces, but evidently also enclosed a parody of it on which Hopkins' sole comment was that at least it assured him that he had understood the meter.

The poem is too long to quote in full—thirty-five eight-line stanzas, which run to some ten pages in the standard text—but a sampling of them will serve to suggest both the rigors and the rewards of the whole.

12

On Saturday sailed from Bremen,
American-outward-bound,
Take settler and seamen, tell men with women,
Two hundred souls in the round—
O Father, not under thy feathers nor ever as guessing
The goal was a shoal, of a fourth the doom to be drowned:
Yet did the dark side of the bay of thy blessing
Not vault them, the millions of rounds of thy mercy not reeve even
them in?

13

Into the snows she sweeps,
    Hurling the haven behind,
The Deutschland, on Sunday; and so the sky keeps,
    For the infinite air is unkind,
And the sea flint-flake, black-backed in the regular blow,
Sitting Eastnortheast, in cursed quarter, the wind;
    Wiry and white-fiery and whirlwind-swivellèd snow
Spins to the widow-making unchilding unfathering deeps.

24

Away in the loveable west,
    On a pastoral forehead of Wales,
I was under a roof here, I was at rest,
    And they the prey of the gales;
She to the black-about air, to the breaker, the thickly
Falling flakes, to the throng that catches and quails
    Was calling, "O Christ, Christ, come quickly":
The cross to her she calls Christ to her, christens her wild-worst
    Best.

34

Now burn, new born to the world,
    Double-naturèd name,
The heaven-flung, heart-fleshed, maiden-furled
    Miracle-in-Mary-of-flame,
Mid-numbered He in three of the thunder-throne!
Not a dooms-day dazzle in his coming nor dark as he came;

> Kind, but royally claiming his own;
> A released shower, let flash to the shire, not a lightning of fire hard-
> hurled.
>
> ### 35
>
> Dame, at our door
> Drowned, and among our shoals,
> Remember us in the roads, the heaven-haven of the Reward:
> Our King back, oh, upon English souls!
> Let him easter in us, be a dayspring to the dimness of us, be a
> crimson-cresseted east,
> More brightening her, rare-dear Britain, as his reign rolls,
> Pride, rose, prince, hero of us, high-priest,
> Our hearts' charity's hearth's fire, our thoughts' chivalry's throng's
> Lord.

"You say you would not for any money read my poem again," he writes. "Nevertheless, I beg you will. Besides money, you know, there is love." It is enough to break the heart. He then goes on to say, "If it is obscure, do not bother yourself with the meaning but pay attention to the best and most intelligible stanzas. . . . If you had done this you would have liked it better and sent me some serviceable criticisms, but now your criticism is of no use, being only a protest memorialising me against my whole policy and proceedings." And then about a year later he touched on the sore subject once more with, "I am sorry you never read the Deutschland again." It is well that at least he did not live to see the letter that his favorite sister, Kate, received from Bridges in 1918, when, some thirty years after Hopkins' death, he was editing the first collection of his friend's poems for publication. "That terrible 'Deutschland' looks and reads much better in type—you will be glad to hear," he wrote her, "but I wish those nuns had stayed at home." In his introduction he puts it this way: "The poem stands logically as well as chronologically in the front of his book, like a great dragon folded in the gate to forbid all entrance."

On the first day of 1888, at St. Stanislaus' College, Tullamore, Hopkins made his last annual retreat, and among his notes on the occasion occurs the following passage:

What is my wretched life? Five wasted years almost have passed in Ireland. I am ashamed of the little I have done, of my waste of time, although my helplessness and weakness is such that I could scarcely do otherwise. . . . All my undertakings miscarry: I am like a straining eunuch. I wish then for death; yet if I died now I should die imperfect, no master of myself, and that is the worst failure of all. O my God, look down on me.

There is nothing convoluted or obscure about that. One almost wishes there were.

I picture him as on some day in 1888 he sat proctoring one of the endless examinations he was responsible for. He is writing in pencil and for paper is using a Royal University of Ireland examination book, which survives to this day. It has various admonitions printed on it like *Write only on the ruled side. Do not write on the margin. No part of this book is to be torn off.* His younger brother Everard—Hopkins was the oldest of nine children—is to be married in April to a girl named Amy Caroline Sichel, and he is trying to compose an epithalamion for their wedding. There is no date on the examination book, but presumably he worked on it sometime during the winter when the examination room was chilly enough for him to wear underneath his black clericals one of the warm things his mother had sent him from England. His gaze is aimed out in the direction of the students bent over their desks in front of him, but it is not the students that he is seeing. Influenced possibly by Edmund Spenser's recurring use of "Sweet Themmes runne softly, till I end my song" in his "Prothalamion," he is seeing instead a river, maybe a particular stretch of one that he knew and used to bathe in near the seminary at Stonyhurst, where he taught for a while before coming to Dublin. In it there was "a deep salmon pool with a funnel of white water at its head which generations of boys had used for a chute," somebody who knew it wrote later.

Directly underneath where the instructions read *The rough work and calculations, as well as the final results, should be shown in this book,* he has written down his poem full of scratched-out words and interlinear corrections.

Hark, hearer, hear what I do; lend a thought now, make believe
We are leaf-whelmed somewhere with the hood
Of some branchy bunchy bushybowered wood,
Southern dean or Lancashire clough or Devon cleave
That leans along the loins of hills, where a candycoloured, where a
*   gluegold-brown*
Marbled river, boisterously beautiful, between

Roots and rocks is danced and dandled, all in froth and
    waterblowballs, down.
We are there, when we hear a shout
That the hanging honeysuck, the dogeared hazels in the cover
Makes dither, makes hover
And the riot of a rout
Of, it must be, boys from the town
Bathing: it is summer's sovereign good.

By there comes a listless stranger: beckoned by the noise
He drops towards the river: unseen
Sees the bevy of them, how the boys
With dare and with downdolphinry and bellbright bodies huddling
    out,
Are earthworld, airworld, waterworld thorough hurled, all by turn
    and turn about.

       •   •   •

This garland of their gambol flashes in his breast
Into such a sudden zest
Of summertime joys
That he hies to a pool neighboring; sees it is the best
There; sweetest, freshest, shadowiest;
Fairyland; silk-beech, scrolled ash, packed sycamore, wild
    wychelm, hornbeam fretty overstood
By. Rafts and rafts of flake-leaves light, dealt so, painted on the air,
Hang as still as hawk or hawkmoth, as the stars or as the angels there,
Like the thing that never knew the earth, never off roots
Rose. Here he feasts: lovely all is! No more: off with—down he dings

His bleachèd both and woolwoven wear:
Careless these in coloured wisp
All lie tumbled-to; then with loop-locks
Forward falling, forehead frowning, lips crisp
Over finger-teasing task, his twiny boots
Fast he opens, last he off wrings
Till walk the world he can with bare his feet
And come where lies a coffer, burly all of blocks
Built of chancequarrièd, selfquainèd hoar-huskèd rocks
And the water warbles over into, filleted with glassy grassy
    quicksilvery shivès and shoots
And with heavenfallen freshness down from moorland still brims,
Dark or daylight, on and on. Here he will then, here he will the fleet
Flinty kindcold element let break across his limbs
Long. Where we leave him, froliclavish, while he looks about him,
    laughs, swims.

• • •

Enough now; since the sacred matter that I mean
I should be wronging longer leaving it to float
Upon this only gambolling and echoing-of-earth note—
What is . . . . the delightful dean?
Wedlock. What the water? Spousal love.

. . . .

to Everard, as I surmise,
Sparkled first in Amy's eyes

. . . .

turns

Father, mother, brothers, sisters, friends

Into fairy trees, wildflowers, woodferns
Rankèd round the bower

. . . .

"Lend a thought now, make believe," he enjoins his hearers, and through long practice he has become so good at make-believe himself that it is as though he is actually there now at the scene he is describing, or at least as much there as he is anywhere as he searches for the words that will bring it to life. He knows what his friends will think, but he cannot resist "dean" instead of "vale," say, or "dell," which would fit the meter equally, because "dean" chimes so well with "cleave" and "leans," as well in fact as "leans" does with "loins," and "cleave with "clough." It is a music that he is always trying for as much as a meaning. But it is the ineluctable look of it that he is trying for too, straining his mind's eye to see it precisely as it was when he knew it. There were times when he used to kneel beside a frozen pond to see the pattern of bubbles trapped under the ice or after a rain crouch on a garden path to study the glitter of crushed quartz before the water evaporated. "Candycoloured" he calls the river, tawny and braided like toffee, then "gluegold-brown," solid and glossy like the glue a bookbinder or a carpenter uses, then "marbled," veined, cool, glinting. A "Marbled river, boisterously beautiful, between / Roots and rocks is danced and dandled, all in froth and waterblowballs, down," he writes with his pencil, hoping that Bridges and the others will forgive him "waterblowballs" on the grounds that there is no ready-made word for what it is that from time to time the air catches out of the froth and tosses free.

But he is listening as well as looking, and above the scratching of pens and the occasional creak of a chair in that chilly, grey-lit room what he hears is a sudden clarion cry, "a shout / That the hanging honeysuck, / The dogeared hazels in the cover / Makes dither, makes hover." It takes him no more than an instant to guess its source—"the riot of a rout / Of, it must be, boys from the town / Bathing: it is summer's sovereign good"—and then there comes a break in the poem as though to make way for the figure of a man approaching to see if he has guessed right.

"By there comes a listless stranger," he says of him, and it is hard to imagine an adjective more richly descriptive of how Hopkins himself must have felt as he sat there at his proctoring—apathetic, without energy, bored, and in terms of the word's Middle English root, "list," which is just the kind of thing Hopkins would have known, *lustless, desireless*. "Beckoned by the noise / He drops towards the river: unseen / Sees the bevy of them, how the boys / With dare and with downdolphinry and bellbright bodies huddling out, / Are earthworld, airworld, waterworld thorough hurled, all by turn and turn about."

"Candycoloured" and "gluegold-brown" minutely describe certain aspects of the river's look if you read them right, but they also have unhelpful associations for twentieth-century readers. In the case of the boys, however, every word remains exactly right. The daredevil, skinny-dipping townies are swift and graceful as the dolphins that according to legend rescue the shipwrecked from drowning the way here they rescue the stranger from his listlessness and solitude. Hidden among the trees, no more listless now than the elders who watched Susanna, he sees the flash of their wet bodies as they leap in and out of the river like bright, bronzed bells ringing wild changes to each other. He watches them with their knees clasped under their chins huddling on the rocks maybe or taking turns at cannonballing off a ledge to leave the world of earth behind for the worlds of air and then water. In their boisterous din and dazzle they are the heart and life of the poem and get its five most magical lines, set apart from the rest, all to themselves. The lines that follow tell how the stranger is heartened and brought to life by them.

As modest and retiring as Hopkins himself, never for an instant does he consider joining them, but finds instead the "sweetest, freshest, shadowiest" of ponds nearby, which is overhung by ash, sycamore, wychelm, hornbeam, with the reflection of their "flake-leaves light" like rafts on the water's surface while the leaves them-selves "Hang as still as hawk or hawkmoth, as the stars or as the angels there, / Like the thing that never knew the earth, never off roots / Rose." The dreamlike, unearthly calm of it after the rout and riot of the boys entrances him as he stands there all by himself: "Here he feasts: lovely all is!" And then the abrupt intrusion of "No more—off with," which rings out as sharp and clarion as the shout that first alerted him to their presence. The shout this time is to himself, and its message is that with the flesh of him starving no less than the spirit, it is no longer enough to feast with only his eyes.

Like Lear crying out "Off, off, you lendings!" because in his inspired madness he knows that only stripped bare will he find his true self and be saved, it is his clothes that the stranger wants off as he stands there at the water's edge. The process of removing them is described with an abundance of detail that would be ludicrous except for the way it suggests that it is part of a sacred ritual. His bleached shirt is the first to go. Next is the "woolwoven wear"— that gift from his mother again?—and "Careless these in coloured wisp / All lie tumbled-to" there on the edge of the pool. Finally, like Moses when he sees that the ground on which he stands is holy, he takes off his shoes, and the process is rendered minutely. "With loop-locks / Forward falling, forehead frowning, lips crisp / Over finger-teasing task" he works at unknotting the laces "Till walk the world he can with bare his feet." Fully naked at last— "Thou art the thing itself!" cries the old king, "poor, bare, forked animal"—he can finally lower himself into the dark pond, "Where we leave him, froliclavish, while he looks about him, laughs, swims."

What confirms the sacramental nature of the undressing is that at the climax of it, immersing himself in the river, he is quite simply transfigured as the "kindcold" water becomes the water of baptism cleansing him, regenerating him, and making him whole. The irony is that what has become for him a means of grace is nothing other than the "bellbright" boys, the trees, the river, and his utterly pagan joy in their beauty.

And then Hopkins suddenly remembers Everard. What he is supposed to be writing is a poem of religious significance appropriate for a priest to give a younger brother on his wedding day. "Enough now," he sternly breaks in upon himself, "since the sacred matter that I mean / I should be wronging longer leaving it to float / Upon this only gambolling and echoing-of-earth note." In other words, Hopkins the priest cannot accept what

Hopkins the poet has conveyed in spite of himself—that the profane is not always the antithesis of the sacred, but sometimes the bearer of it, and that the echoing-of-earth note he has struck is precisely what gives his poem its most profoundly religious resonance. Instead, dutifully, he tries to turn the whole thing into an allegory.

"What is . . . the delightful dean? / Wedlock. What the water? Spousal love." There is a gap in the manuscript here as though he knows perfectly well that it is not working and leaves room for fixing it later. Then after the only scrap of doggerel he was ever guilty of—"to Everard, as I surmise, / Sparkled first in Amy's eyes"—he sinks still deeper into the morass as he switches his attention to the guests who will be showing up at the ceremony that April and "turns / Father, mother, brothers, sisters, friends / Into fairy trees, wildflowers, woodferns / Rankèd round the bower . . ." At this point he sets his pencil aside and leaves the poem an unfinished fragment.

Not by a long shot, however, are unfinished fragments all that he managed to produce those Dublin years. There is also a handful of poems that, as he told Bridges in a letter, came to him "like inspirations unbidden and against my will." He said he would be sending them along shortly, but he never did, and as a result it was not until after his death that Bridges finally came across them in a large bundle of miscellaneous papers dispatched to him by a university colleague, Father Thomas Wheeler, who had taken care of Hopkins during his last illness. It was Bridges who called them the "terrible sonnets," meaning marked by "terrible pathos," as another of Hopkins literary correspondents, Richard Dixon, had said of his poetry in general, and nothing else Hopkins ever wrote is so nakedly and painfully self-revelatory. It is no wonder that he could not bring himself to show them to even his closest and most faithful friends. They are poems in which, by facing the worst of his darkness with almost unbearable honesty, he manages somehow to face it down, to survive it. But what gives them greater power still is that at the same time they speak for, speak to, speak about all those who in some measure have faced the same darkness themselves.

I wake and feel the fell of dark, not day.
What hours, O what black hours we have spent
This night! what sights you, heart, saw; ways you went!
And more must, in yet longer light's delay.

With witness I speak this. But where I say
Hours I mean years, mean life. And my lament
Is cries, countless, cries like dead letters sent
To dearest him that lives alas! away.

I am gall. I am heartburn. God's most deep decree
Bitter would have me taste: my taste was me;
Bones built in me, flesh filled, blood brimmed the curse.

Self-yeast of spirit a dull dough sours. I see
The lost are like this, and their scourge to be
As I am mine, their sweating selves; but worse.

Here it is literal darkness that is the starting point. He wakes up in the small third-floor room that he occupied in Newman House at the university thinking that it must be day only to discover to his horror not just that it is still night, but a night so dense that he can all but feel the "fell" of it. "Fell" means *pelt*, suggesting night as a vast, shaggy beast looming over him, but it also means *cruel, savage, ruthless,* and beyond that, as a noun, means an upland waste or sheer cliff, which is to say a perilous and terrifying place to be at any time, let alone when you can't see the hand in front of your face, a place where at any moment you may *fall*, literally or figuratively, or be *felled* by an unseen enemy. Again and again Hopkins chooses words open to so many interpretations that, like prisms when the light touches them, they cast across the page a whole spectrum of possible meanings.

He lies there in the dark for what seem hours, and in his desperate wakefulness sees sights and travels ways that make him dread the hours still to come before day finally breaks. Or rather, he says, it is his heart that has seen them, has forced them upon him, as though he and his heart are in desperate, unresolvable conflict, as though his heart is as much the enemy within as the shaggy beast is the enemy without, and that is what makes their hours together so black. Who knows what the sights and ways he refers to were, but who, having lain sleepless like that, can fail to know? "I realize that from the cradle up I have been like the rest of the race—never quite sane in the night," Mark Twain wrote in his autobiography, and part of the insanity is to relive endless scenes of failure and loss until finally an entire lifetime is seen in all its ways as hopelessly benighted.

"Yea, the darkness hideth not from thee; but the night shineth as the day," says the 139th Psalm, and that or something like it was likely in the back of Hopkins' mind when he wrote "With witness I say this" at the start of the second quatrain. Who else but God or Christ could witness a depth of anguish so profound and personal that he kept it hidden not just from his Jesuit colleagues, who never seem to have guessed the full extent of it, but from even the family and friends dearest to him? Presumably he chose to hide it from them for the same reason he chose also to hide sonnets like this one, which do not so much describe the anguish as they embody it, *are* it. Nor was it just the sleepless nights in the small room that God witnessed, but all the years of his life, all the times he had cried out in the dark to the one who, for all his witnessing, either ignored his awful need or failed to recognize it. "Like dead letters / Sent to dearest him that lives alas! away" is the way he describes his unheeded prayers, and it is a devastating image to come from anyone, let alone from this man whose fifteen Jesuit years had been centered beyond all else on praying. There was a time when he had written of Christ in relation to humankind as "Their ransom, their rescue, and first, fast, last friend," and now he found himself friendless. What makes the image more moving still are the roots that it seems to have had deep in Hopkins' past.

When he was a twenty-year-old undergraduate at Oxford, he met a young man several years his junior the memory of whom was to remain with him for the rest of his life. Digby Dolben was the young man's name, and in February of 1865 he was visiting Robert Bridges, a distant cousin, in hopes of entering Oxford himself in a year or two. Balliol was the college he had chosen, and since Bridges was a Corpus man himself, he introduced the young man to his classmate Hopkins, who, as a member of Balliol, would show him around the place and perhaps help him eventually get in. Tall, slender, pale, with a dreaming quality about his eyes—at Hopkins' request he sent him a carte de visite photograph some months later—he wrote poetry and was so fascinated by Roman Catholicism that while still at Eton he took to walking around the countryside barefoot and dressed in the robes of a monk. The two of them never saw each other again after those few days together in Oxford, but in one sense or another Hopkins seems to have lost his heart to him. When he learned of his death three years later—he drowned trying to save a child he was teaching to swim in the river Welland—he wrote Bridges, "There can very seldom have happened the loss of so much beauty (in body and mind and life) and of the promise of still more as there has been in his case."

But throughout their brief relationship, Hopkins apparently had a sense of guilt about his feelings for him. He notes in his diary that it is dangerous to think about him, and if his name came up in conversation, he quickly backed away from it. "Running on in thought last night unseasonably against warning onto subject of Dolben," one entry reads and "Going on into a letter to Dolben at night agst. warning" reads another, warnings presumably that came from the priest who had confessed him. And then something apparently happened that further shadowed their relationship. It has been suggested that overtly or otherwise Hopkins may have made his feelings known to Dolben in a way that the boy was unable or unwilling to respond to—who knows?—but for whatever reason there seems to have been some kind of breach between them. "Give my love to him [another friend] and Dolben," he says to Bridges. "I have written letters without end to the latter without a whiff of an answer," letters that all those years later he was reminded of by the fruitless prayers.

All his life he was troubled by the feelings stirred in him at the sight of male beauty. Temptation was everywhere, and in his diaries he takes frequent note of it—a glance from another man that lingered a fraction of a second too long, a beautiful boy in the choir at Magdalen, "looking with terrible attention at Maitland" or at students walking in Christ Church meadows, the charm of some street child seen from the hidden vantage of a shop door. During his devotions, even the contemplation of Christ's body on the cross disturbed him. In other words, if on the one hand the memory of his love for Dolben helped dispel the darkness a little, much as the bathing boys dispelled the stranger's listlessness, on the other hand it plunged him into the darkness even deeper still both because of what he considered shameful about that love and, even worse in his eyes, because of his sadness and regret at never having fulfilled it. Either he had never found the courage so much as to tell Dolben how he felt, or, if in some way he possibly did, he had all but destroyed their friendship in the process. "Dearest him" was the boy he had loved and lost and at the same time the God whom he believed he had lost no less, both of them as dead to him as dead letters and farther away than the farthest star.

The sestet is quite simply a description of hell. Gall and heartburn are not the disease he has but the disease he is, and in the bitterness of despair, abandonment, self-loathing, he recognizes that it is nothing other than himself that he is tasting. Bitterer still is his recognition that it is by "God's most deep decree" that this has come to pass, and thus it is impossible for him either to fathom it fully or to question its justice. In an earlier version of the sonnet he writes less elliptically, "my bones build, my flesh fills, blood feeds / This curse"—God's curse on Adam for his sin—and Hopkins says that for him, as for the rest of the lost, the essence of the torment, the cruelest sting of the scourge, is simply, hopelessly, endlessly, to be his sweating, self-tormenting, dull, and self-souring self. And then the terrible thud of the final "But worse." It is unclear whether he means that it is for himself alone or for the lost in general that there is worse still to come, but, either way, he ends, as he begins, with such unrelenting darkness that in all probability this is the poem he meant when he wrote to Bridges, "I have after long silence written two sonnets, which I am touching; if ever anything was written in blood one of these was."

It was not all darkness, of course. Life went on. In the summers of 1885 and 1886 Hopkins paid visits to his family in England. He attended some London galleries with his painter brother Arthur, spent a few days renewing old ties in Oxford, and for the first time met Bridges' new wife, who charmed him. A younger teaching colleague named Robert Curtis became a friend, and together they went to Wales on a vacation with twenty pounds from the rector to cover their expenses—Hopkins lamented that they returned with eight pounds of it still unspent. "A delightful holiday," he calls it in a letter to Bridges despite the fact that there was a good deal of bad weather. They took walks for sometimes as much as twenty or thirty miles through the rough Welsh countryside. He made a pencil sketch of the Glaslyn River, "a torrent of notably green water . . . the beauty of which is unsurpassed," in Portmadoc saw Bretons in jerseys, earrings, and wooden shoes selling vegetables, and spent a week in Caernarfon with its great Edward I castle. Summing things up to his mother, he wrote, "We had much rain but did well nevertheless. We got no seabathing. I preached two little sermons. The holiday has been a new life to me."

But the darkness seems to have persisted even so, as if it had been home to him for so long that he was almost reluctant to leave it. In notes he made for a meditation on hell some years earlier he wrote of a member of the damned as "gnawing and feeding on its own most miserable self," and despite the holidays, the friends, and the pleasure he never stopped taking in the beauties of the earth, he seems to have taken a kind of grim pleasure in the darkness as well. It was like feeding on his own decaying flesh, his own decaying faith, and it is with that macabre image that he begins what Bridges believed to be the second of the two "bloody" sonnets.

> Not, I'll not, carrion comfort, Despair, not feast on thee;
> Not untwist—slack they may be—these last strands of man
> In me or, most weary, cry I can no more. I can;
> Can something, hope, wish day come, not choose not to be.
>
> But ah, but O thou terrible, why wouldst thou rude on me
> Thy wring-world right foot rock? lay a lionlimb against me? scan
> With darksome devouring eyes my bruisèd bones? and fan,
> O in turns of tempest, me heaped there; me frantic to avoid thee and
>   flee?

Why? That my chaff might fly; my grain lie, sheer and clear.
Nay in all that toil, that coil, since (seems) I kissed the rod,
Hand rather, my heart lo! lapped strength, stole joy, would laugh,
    cheer.
Cheer whom though? The hero whose heaven-handling flung me,
    foot trod
Me? or me that fought him? O which one? is it each one? That
    night, that year
Of now done darkness I wretch lay wrestling with (my God!)
    my God.

What he is talking about in this breathless, ragged poem is both the worst and the best that have happened to him. The best he saves for the final line, where we learn that the darkness is "now done" in the sense of over and done with. That is the point from which the rest of the poem is a flashback, and yet he touches on it so lightly that all but a careful reader might miss it altogether. Instead, it is the darkness itself that he continues to be obsessed by, like a man who, even after he has recovered from a terrible illness, is unable to talk about anything else. At worst it even tempted him to suicide, and only by an enormous effort of the will did he manage to resist crying out "I can no more" in the words of Shakespeare's Marc Antony falling on his sword. What saved him was only "something"—something like the faint hope, as he lay sleepless in his bed, that day might come, only that one small, pathetic wish because to wish for anything grander was beyond him. It was beyond him too to choose, actively and affirmatively, to go on living a life that had become unbearable. The most he could do was at least not choose not to. It was a negative little victory at best, but at least it saved the day for him. And yet, again, it is not the day and the being saved that he focuses on, but the horror that he was saved from.

It was God who was at the heart of it, or absent at the heart of it, the God who had abandoned him. "O thou terrible" he calls him, and then follows a series of images that it must have shaken him to his foundations to utter, that most devout and dedicated man. It was not just a poem he was writing, but an indictment.

God is a cosmic bully and tyrant. "The earth is my footstool," God says to Isaiah, but here the great foot is on Hopkins' own godforsaken neck. It is not just pinning him down, but rocking back and forth as if to crush him like an insect.

God is a ravening beast. Possibly echoing Revelation's "'The lion of the tribe of Judah . . . has conquered" or Isaiah's "like a lion he breaks all my bones," he says that God laid his "lionlimb" "against" him in the sense not just of "upon him," but of "doing battle with him," as light does battle with dark, good with evil. At the same time, God "scans" him, searches him to his nethermost depths, with "darksome, devouring eyes." It is the same fearsome beast, of course, whose shaggy fell he woke to feel in the impenetrable night.

God is a winnowing fan. But then, as in a nightmare, the fan whips the air into such a tempest that he is as helpless before it as a heap of grain and as desperate to escape as the psalmist fleeing to the uttermost parts of the sea.

When Job cried out "Why hast thou made me thy mark?" you can imagine the sound of it rending the heavens, but after the violent staccato of the earlier lines Hopkins' single, shuddering "Why?" at the start of the sestet seems almost a whisper. The way he answers his own question, on the other hand, could hardly be more Job-like. "Though he slay me, yet will I trust in him," says the man of Uz, and out of a faith no less transcendent for all its battering the man of Dublin says that he has come to see at last that the darksome, devouring-eyed one, the lion, the breaker and bruiser of bones, the tempest, was all the time working toward one beatific end, which was "That my chaff might fly; my grain lie, sheer and clear." One can only hope that it marked the turning point not only of his poem, but of his life.

"Whom the Lord loveth, he chasteneth," says the Epistle to the Hebrews, and once Hopkins found it possible both to discern the love behind the chastening and also to believe in it, once he was able to kiss the rod together with the hand that wielded it, day dawned for him at long last and everything changed. His heart "lapped strength," he says, as if he knelt at the "boisterously beautiful" river in "Epithalamion" to drink, as if he remembered the psalmist's "As the hart panteth after the water brooks, so panteth my soul after thee." You wonder whether the last picture of the listless stranger bathing in that river was in some way a metaphor for this moment: "Here he will the fleet / Flinty kindcold element let break across his limbs / Long. Where we leave him, froliclavish, while he looks about him, laughs, swims." In any event, there came a moment when the carrion comfort of despair was somehow routed, and, strong of heart, "he stole joy, would laugh, cheer."

Maybe the phrase "stole joy" should make us uneasy—as though he sees his deliverance less as something that God of his mercy gave him than as something he took for himself while God was looking the other way. But in the meanwhile, with the little pause that comes in the midst of the spondee created by "cheer" at the end of one line and then again at the start of the next, it is as if Hopkins is pausing to savor the joy and laughter and cheering for as long as they last, possibly even to remember the poems, they gave rise to before the shadows gathered.

> The world is charged with the grandeur of God.
> It will flame out, like shining from shook foil;
> It gathers to a greatness, like the ooze of oil
> Crushed. Why do men then now not reck his rod?
> Generations have trod, have trod, have trod;
> And all is seared with trade; bleared, smeared with toil;
> And wears man's smudge and shares man's smell: the soil
> Is bare now, nor can foot feel, being shod.
>
> • • •
>
> And for all this, nature is never spent;
> There lives the dearest freshness deep down things;
> And though the last lights off the black West went
> Oh, morning, at the brown brink eastward, springs—
> Because the Holy Ghost over the bent
> World broods with warm breast and with ah! bright wings.

Well before Dublin, in other words, he knew that the world was bent and that night was coming, but he knew also that, even in the thick of it, Christ was present. The poem he wrote about it he called "The Lantern out of Doors."

Sometimes a lantern moves along the night
That interests our eyes. And who goes there?
I think; where from and bound, I wonder, where,
With, all down darkness wide, his wading light?

Men go by me whom either beauty bright
In mould or mind or what not else makes rare:
They rain against our much-thick and marsh air
Rich beams, till death or distance buys them quite.

Death or distance soon consumes them: wind
What most I may eye after, be in at the end
I cannot, and out of sight is out of mind.

Christ minds: Christ's interest, what to avow or amend
There, eyes them, heart wants, care haunts, foot follows kind,
Their ransom, their rescue, and first, fast, last friend.

He wrote these poems—in fact about a third of his entire body of work—during the three years, from 1874 to 1877, that he spent studying theology at St. Beuno's College overlooking the lovely valley of the Elwy and the Clwyd in North Wales, and perhaps never again was his life so happy or his faith so unshadowed and unquestioning. It was not just in the beauty of the Welsh country-side that he saw God's grandeur, but in virtually everything and everybody. He was fascinated by what he called "instress" or "inscape"—the essential individuality and particularity of things, what his beloved Duns Scotus called their *hæcceity*—which in the case of human beings, in, what he believed it to be was their deeply buried likeness to Christ.

> As kingfishers catch fire, dragonflies draw flame;
> As tumbled over rim in roundy wells
> Stones ring; like each tucked string tells, each hung bell's
> Bow swung finds tongue to fling out broad its name;
> Each mortal thing does one thing and the same:
> Deals out that being indoors each one dwells;
> Selves—goes itself; myself it speaks and spells,
> Crying What I do is me: for that I came.
>
> I say more: the just man justices;
> Keeps grace: that keeps all his goings graces;
> Acts in God's eye what in God's eye he is—
> Christ. For Christ plays in ten thousand places,
> Lovely in limbs, and lovely in eyes not his
> To the Father through the features of men's faces.

In "The Windhover," which he called "the best thing I ever wrote," he sees Christ even in the flight of a bird.

> I caught this morning's minion, kingdom of daylight's dauphin,
>   dapple-dawn-drawn Falcon, in his riding
> Of the rolling level underneath him steady air, and striding
> High there, how he rung upon the rein of a wimpling wing
> In his ecstasy! then off, off forth on swing,

As a skate's heel sweeps smooth on a bow-bend: the hurl and
*   gliding*
Rebuffed the big wind. My heart in hiding
Stirred for a bird—the achieve of, the mastery of the thing!

Brute beauty and valour and act, oh, air, pride, plume, here
Buckle! AND the fire that breaks from thee then, a billion
Times told lovelier, more dangerous, O my chevalier!

No wonder of it: sheer plod makes plough down sillion
Shine, and blue-bleak embers, ah my dear,
Fall, gall themselves, and gash gold-vermilion.

The bird—a kestrel, or *falco tinnunculus*—is sometimes called a windhover because of its uncanny ability to remain stationary over one spot by flying into the wind at precisely the wind's speed, beating its quivering ("wimpling") wings more slowly as the gusts diminish and more rapidly as they pick up again. After the hover, if nothing catches its eye on the ground, it banks against the wind like a skater heeling around a bend or speeds down-wind on the "rolling level underneath him steady air" until with a sudden about turn and upward swoop or "stride" it resumes its hovering. If it spots quarry, it makes a sloping descent with wings held high and tense above its back. Along with many other readers I take the difficult word "buckle" to refer, among other things, to this downward maneuver, which it seems to me is at the heart of the poem's meaning, as it is evoked also by the parallel images of the last three lines. It is when the "sheer plod" of the plowman presses the plow-share down hard into the furrow that burnishes it that the metal shines brightest. It is in falling and galling (in the sense of *breaking* or *wounding*) themselves that the blue-bleak embers reveal the splendor of the fire within. It is Christ in his glory that is repre-sented by the bird in the full majesty of flight, but more glorious still is the incarnation, when, like the bird buckling, Christ descends into the world's suffering to be born in a stable and die on a cross between thieves for the world's sake.

To return to "Carrion Comfort," written some eight or ten years later, once Hopkins realized there in the bleakness of Dublin that the lion-limbed God he addressed as "O thou terrible" was not his enemy but his savior and friend, his heart among other things "cheered," and what the cheering was all about was the same vic-tory through defeat, finding through losing, life through death, self-fulfillment through self-immolation, that "The Windhover" had celebrated in years gone by. He cheers God in "Carrion Comfort" because at the heart of "now done darkness" he has dis-covered light as effulgent as fire at the heart of an ember, and dur-ing the catch of breath between this "cheer" at the end of one line and the other "cheer" at the start of the next, it is as if for a moment he savors the laughter and joy of the discovery. But then as a kind of grim afterthought the second "cheer" comes. "Cheer whom then?" he asks, and in answering his own question he invokes the image of Jacob and God wrestling in the black of night on the banks of the river Jabbok. Is it God he is cheering, he asks—cheer-ing him for the "heaven-handling" that in the midst of spiritual death has given him new life, as Jacob was given a new name and a new destiny to go with it by the one who leapt upon him out of the darkness. Or is he cheering himself for having dared to take on such an adversary? Can it be that he is cheering both? Whatever the answer, it is the darkness rather than the light that the poem ends with, the God who wrestles rather than the God who saves. The darkness may have been over and done with, but he was still devastated by it.

Hopkins was in the last few years of his life and in frail health both physically and mentally, but he continued with his professional duties including the endless examinations, worked at a paper on free will, which like many other projects he put away unfinished, tried to compose some music as best he could with no piano available to him for trying it out on. He made some sketches. He played a retaliatory practical joke on an acquaintance, writing an appropriately crude and misspelled letter purporting to be from the son of a livery stableman in search of a job on a Dublin newspaper, and when the acquaintance fell for it, he was rapturous: "I could not have believed in such a success nor that life had this pleasure to bestow." His behavior became increasingly eccentric. A hostess found him waiting for her in the drawing room seated in front of the fire with his jacket off as he sewed up a rip in his waistcoat, and the story is that he was once, unimaginably, discovered blowing pepper through a keyhole to break up a meeting that for some reason or another he found objectionable. He attended a concert at which one Herr Slapoffski ("real name") played a Handel violin concerto. And he continued to write some poetry.

In the fall of 1888 he was asked to write a poem in honor of a Spanish saint, canonized only the year before, whose first feast day was imminent, and he sent an early version of it to Bridges along with the acerbic comment: "The sonnet (I say it snorting) aims at being intelligible." Alphonsus Rodriguez was the saint's name, a sixteenth-century Jesuit lay brother who for some forty years served as hall porter at the college of Montesion in Palma de Mallorca and whose fragmentary spiritual writings have much to say of his constant battling with demonic visions that threatened both his faith and his chastity. Hopkins, during his novitiate in Manresa House, Roehampton, had been a porter himself for a few months, and the log he kept at the time is full of the same details of illness, rotation of personnel, changes in daily routine, and the like that must have occupied porters down through the centuries.

Honour is flashed off exploit, so we say;
And those strokes once that gashed flesh or galled shield
Should tongue that time now, trumpet now that field,
And, on the fighter, forge his glorious day.
On Christ they do and on the martyr may;
But be the war within, the brand we wield
Unseen, the heroic breast not outward-steeled,
Earth hears no hurtle then from fiercest fray.
Yet God (that hews mountain and continent,
Earth, all, out; who, with trickling increment,
Veins violets and tall trees makes more and more)
Could crowd career with conquest while there went
Those years and years by of world without event
That in Majorca Alfonso watched the door.

It is not hard to imagine all the ways in which Hopkins identified with his subject. Like Alphonsus Rodriguez, he had lived a life that could hardly have seemed more uneventful, more drab, unfulfilled, wasted. In another of his last few sonnets he wrote, "birds build—but not I build; no, but strain, / Time's eunuch, and not breed one work that wakes. / Mine, O thou lord of life, send my roots rain," and it seems clear that it was more than just his literary work that he was thinking about, the failure of his poems to wake much enthusiasm in anybody. "All my undertakings miscarry: I am like a straining eunuch," he wrote Bridges at about this time, and clearly what he is thinking about is his life as a whole.

In the various parishes he had served—in London and in the slums of Liverpool and Glasgow among others—he had been effective neither as a preacher nor as a pastor and knew it. In Dublin his students found his classes for the most part dull and irrelevant. He never produced anything of much significance either in his musical compositions or his sketches, and the innumerable scholarly papers that he started were rarely completed. Far more personally and painfully, the passionate longing that he had felt his whole life for the beauty he saw in the boys in the river and all the others they represented, including of course Digby Dolben, the "dearest him that lives alas! away," had gone unfulfilled because in his world, in his calling, to have in any way sought to fulfill it would have been simply unthinkable. In other words it was everything that he had ever done, everything he had ever been, that seemed as pointless and profitless as Alphonso's forty years of watching the door. Yet in the sonnet he wrote to honor him, he saw something more than that, and saw it not just in the saint, it would seem, but also in himself.

In "Carrion Comfort" he asks the question whether in his Jacob-like wrestling with God it is perhaps not God that he should be cheering, but himself for daring to take God on, and here he looks more deeply into the nature of the struggle, into what it means to win, what it means to lose. The world honors those who, like Christ and his martyrs, wear the outward and visible signs of their heroism—the gashed flesh, the galled shield—but the world has no way of even knowing about let alone honoring people like Alphonsus Rodriguez, whose struggles not just with their demons but with none other than God are no less fierce and heroic for being entirely unseen and unguessed. When *The Strange Case of Dr. Jekyll and Mr. Hyde* first came out, Hopkins wrote Bridges, "You are certainly wrong about Hyde being overdrawn; my Hyde is worse," and it is hard not to believe that it was of his own demons and his own battle that he was thinking as he wrote of the saint's.

The poem's loveliest lines fall within the long parenthesis in the sestet. By placing them there, it is as though he makes no claim to know anything overarching or substantive about the mystery of God's dealings with the human race, but in a kind of awestruck aside is simply declaring, just loud enough to hear, what seems to him the infinite patience with which God brings into being everything there is, from the veined petals of violets to the immensity of continents. And then, in the last three lines, comes the climactic revelation that it is this same God who out of what seemed the utterly insignificant life of a doorkeeper was year after year, slowly and painstakingly, bringing into being a great hero of the faith. Is it too much to hope that Hopkins may have at least momentarily considered the possibility that God had been at work in his own life toward the same end?

He had not chosen not to be. He had not succumbed either to despair or to the Hyde within. He had performed his duties faithfully. With little or no encouragement from anybody he had managed to write a few poems. If nothing else, he had *survived*. Is it possible that during those last bleak months of his life he caught at least a glimpse of how maybe in time the world would come to honor him for the work he had done and the battle he had fought? One can only hope that in some such way, however fleetingly, his roots were sent rain.

My own heart let me more have pity on; let
Me live to my sad self hereafter kind,
Charitable; not live this tormented mind
With this tormented mind tormenting yet.
I cast for comfort I can no more get
By groping round my comfortless, than blind
Eyes in their dark can day or thirst can find
Thirst's all-in-all in all a world of wet.

Soul, self; come, poor Jackself, I do advise
You, jaded, let be; call off thoughts awhile
Elsewhere; leave comfort root-room; let joy size
At God knows when to God knows what; whose smile
's not wrung, see you; unforeseen times rather—as skies
Betweenpie mountains—lights a lovely mile.

It is impossible to establish the chronological sequence of the "terrible sonnets," but it is tempting to believe that this least terrible of them was the last, suggesting as it does that there came a time when he finally found a new understanding both of himself and of the way God is present in the creation. Even his tone of voice seems new—quieter, calmer, as easy and heart-to-heart in the sestet as a friend talking to a friend. "My sad self," he says, and in that one small adjective all the misery of the Dublin years is compacted and somehow made manageable, as if for once he is able to stand back from it and see, among other things, how much smaller it really was than what he has for so long been making of it. In letters to Bridges he wrote things like "that coffin of weakness and dejection in which I live" and "I think that my fits of sadness, though they do not affect my judgment, resemble madness," which sound almost operatic by comparison.

He says with equal understatement that to have pity on his own heart means simply to be as kind and charitable to himself as Christ calls all of us to be to our neighbors, with the implication that unless charity begins at home, the chances are that there will be something a little grim and bloodless about it everywhere else.

In "I wake and feel the fell of dark," he wrote, "The lost are like this, and their scourge to be / as I am mine, their sweating selves," and here in enjoining himself not to "live this tormented mind / With this tormented mind tormenting yet" he says it again, but once more he seems to be stepping back far enough to see that all his years of hyperscrupulosity and self-flagellation were, among other things, a little absurd and obsessive, as absurd in fact as the nagging repetition of "tormented," "tormented," "tormenting" in the space of hardly more than a single line. As absurd as trying to find comfort when it is precisely comfortlessness that he has long been determined to inflict upon himself, and as absurd as trying to quench the thirst that rises from the depths of the soul with *water* of all things. And the mad babble of "all" three times in a row serves to point up the madness of what he has spent his life doing to himself. At last he seems to see that the "O thou terrible" of "Carrion Comfort" has all along been none other than himself.

In the sestet he becomes his own Dutch uncle, speaking to himself with a kind of deprecatory affection as "poor Jackself"—Jack as in "All work and no play makes Jack a dull boy," jack-of-all-trades, jack-tar—drudging, unappreciated, dull old Jack. And *"poor"* Jackself, "poor" with all the pity in it of Lear's "Poor fool and knave, I have one part in my heart that's sorry yet for thee," as he and his jester take refuge together from the pitiless storm. "Jaded" brings back "listless," as the stranger was when the noise of the bathing boys beckoned him down to the river years before. And then he reduces to two syllables the best advice that he has it in him either to give or to hear—"Let be," as in *let go, let happen, let lie, let live.* "Call off thoughts awhile," he says, as you call off yammering dogs, and the thoughts he means, that most inward-looking and self-analytic of men, are of course thoughts about himself. Call them off "elsewhere," meaning *anywhere* in the sense that any blessed thing in the world would be more profitable for him to think about than his own endlessly yammering predicament. Instead of groping around like a blind man for some comfort of his own manufacture—some comforting belief, or prayer, or friend, or memory—he tells himself simply to let comfort happen the way flowers happen when properly rooted. More than mere comfort, he tells himself to let "joy" happen—let joy "size," in the sense of *grow*, at a time and to a size that God alone will determine, and the words "God knows when" and "God knows what" become a kind of helpless rolling of the eyes at God's elusiveness and unpredictability.

There is no way to know when joy will happen or what will occasion it, only that there is no way to make it happen because then it would not be God's joy. It is not wrung like a promise or an admission. Instead—and suddenly Hopkins the coiner of outlandish words is the one who is speaking again—it is "unforeseen times," like the time he saw the "dapple-dawn-drawn" bird hovering in the sky above him or the "flame-bright" passage of the dragonfly, or heard the shout from the river or the ringing of stones tumbled into a well, or finally received the long awaited letter.

The final image of "unforeseen times," of God's unwrung smile, is both so vivid and so full of hope that one can only pray that this was indeed the last of the sonnets "written in blood" and that it gives us a glimpse of what Hopkins finally found on the far side of darkness. The smile comes unbidden and unexpected the way sometimes a ray of sun will break through clouds to "betweenpie mountains," meaning that, although the mountains are still in shadow, the space between them is pied, dappled, with light. It may not seem all that much at any given time, but it is enough. At the very least it "lights a lovely mile" of the road—wherever in the world the road may be leading to next.

Hopkins contracted typhoid in the spring of 1889. He was moved to another building and a lighter, less drafty room where there was a nurse to help take care of him. "The only complaint I have to make," he wrote his mother, "is that food and medicine keep coming in like cricket balls." It pleased him that his sickness got him out of correcting examinations during the busiest part of the academic year, although he knew, he said, that there would be the devil to pay later. In earlier days, when his illnesses had been at least in part psychosomatic, he had groused a good deal, but now, he wrote his mother again, "I am the placidest soul in the world," and it seems to have been so.

For a period of about two weeks he showed such marked improvement that Father Wheeler, a fellow priest who was taking care of him, wrote his family and Bridges that he seemed to be out of danger altogether. But Hopkins himself apparently had the feeling that he was not going to recover, and on June 5 he took such a turn for the worse that his parents were summoned from England. On the morning of Saturday, June 8, Father Wheeler administered the Viaticum to him—*Accipe, frater, Viaticum corporis Jesu Christi*—and when everybody at his bedside could see that he was not going to pull through, it was followed by extreme unction. Those who were there with him believed that his mind remained perfectly clear to the end, and at several points they heard him whisper, "I am so happy, I am so happy," which seem to have been his final words.

A few years ago my wife and I made the long, depressing drive through the trafficky streets of north Dublin to the cemetery of Glasnevin, where Hopkins is buried. The cemetery itself is huge, with an overpowering monument to O'Connell and his fellow Irish patriots together with a great many other lesser ones scattered around among the various paths, but the Jesuits' plot is quite small and surrounded by an iron picket fence painted white. Instead of grass, it is covered with pebbles, and the effect is dreary and antiseptic. None of the many densely crowded graves beneath our feet, including Hopkins', was marked in any way, but there is a sizable granite cross toward the center on whose base some two hundred names are carved, including "P. GERARDUS HOPKINS OBIIT JUN. 8 1889 AETAT. AN. 44.

Translated from the Latin, the official notice of his death in the Jesuits' register says, "On the eighth day of June, the vigil of Pentecost, weakened by fever, he rested. May he rest in peace. He had a most subtle mind, which too quickly wore out the fragile strength of his body." Reading it is to be reminded of Katharine Tynan's description of him as he looked in the studio of J. B. Yeats three years earlier, when they met for the first time: "small and childish-looking, yet like a child-sage, nervous too and very sensitive, with a small ivory pale face."

PART 2

MARK TWAIN:
THE MAN WHO WAS NEVER
QUITE SANE IN THE NIGHT

Mark Twain, like his near contemporary Gerard Manley Hopkins, was a slender, narrow-shouldered man, on the short side, with a head that looked slightly too large for his body. His magnificently unruly shock of hair, auburn in youth and eventually white as snow, made him seem taller than he was and "tilted from side to side in his undulating walk," as William Dean Howells describes it in *My Mark Twain*, which of all the portraits we have of him is the most touching and in many ways seems to ring truest. "He glimmered at you from the narrow slits of fine blue-greenish eyes, under branching brows, which with age grew more and more like a sort of plumage," Howells goes on to say, and then adds the most haunting part of his description: "He was apt to smile into your face with a subtle but amiable perception, and yet with a sort of remote absence; you were all there for him, but he was not all there for you."

What is haunting about it, of course, is the question it leaves you with: Where was the part of him that was not there, not even for as old and dear a friend as Howells? From what we have come to know about him both through what he wrote and through the countless volumes written about him, the answer seems to be that it inhabited much the same kind of interior space that Hopkins describes in his last poems. "With the going down of the sun my

faith failed and the clammy fears gathered about my heart," Twain
wrote in his autobiography. "Those were awful nights, nights of
despair, nights charged with the bitterness of death." And later, "In
my age as in my youth, night brings me many a deep remorse. I
realize that from the cradle up I have been like the rest of the
human race—never quite sane in the night."

The popular version of his life story is as familiar as the stories he
spent much of that life writing. Born Samuel Langhorne Clemens
in Florida, Missouri, in 1835, a few years later he was taken by his
parents to the river town of Hannibal, where he spent his boyhood
having many of the same kinds of adventures among many of the
same kinds of people that he later described in *Tom Sawyer* and
Huckleberry Finn. At the age of twelve, when his father died, he left
school to be apprenticed to a printer and ended up writing various
kinds of articles and sketches for his older brother Orion's newspaper. One thing led to another, and some ten years later he became
the pilot of a Mississippi River steamboat, a career he continued to
pursue until it was brought to an end by the outbreak of the Civil
War. Drifting west then in the wake of Orion, who had been
appointed secretary to the governor of the Nevada Territory, he
worked at mining silver for a while and eventually joined the staff of
the Virginia City *Territorial Enterprise*, where as a journalist he first
started using his immortal pseudonym. From that point on he rose
more or less steadily to fame and fortune as humorist, novelist, lec-
turer, and citizen of the world, until it reached the point where he
had only to enter a restaurant wearing his celebrated white suit for
everybody to stand up and applaud. Oxford gave him an honorary
doctorate, along with Auguste Rodin, General William Booth of

the Salvation Army, and Rudyard Kipling; Kaiser Wilhelm seated him at his right hand at dinner; even the New England literary establishment as represented by the likes of Emerson and Longfellow came to accept him; and full of honors and universally loved, he died in his bed with Halley's comet, which had hailed his birth seventy-five years earlier, once again blazing in the night sky. But there was another very different kind of story to tell about another very different kind of man, and it was undoubtedly Howells' at least partial knowledge of both that lay behind his description of that smile, which, for all its glimmering, blue-eyed amiability, kept much hidden, including among other things the secret of his shadowed childhood.

John Marshall Clemens, his Virginia-born father, was on the one hand a leading citizen of Hannibal—chairman of committees, superintendent of road surveying, promoter of the scheme to build a railroad west to the Kansas border—and as the town's Justice of the Peace was known and respected as Judge Clemens. On the other hand he was a man born to failure. His various attempts as a landlord and owner of a dry-goods store to support his wife and, at one point, seven children were so perpetually unsuccessful that, in order to satisfy his creditors, he was forced to sell his Hannibal real estate including the family home, and his son Sam was haunted all his life by the fear of falling into poverty and pauperdom like him. Judge Clemens did the best he knew how for his children—once in a while read poetry to them in a toneless voice and occasionally bought them a book or two, going even so far as to subscribe for them to an illustrated publication called *Peter Parley's Magazine*, which the older ones adored—but grim, stern, harried, and aloof as he was, he spent little or no time with them, and Sam claimed that he could not remember ever having seen him laugh and only once saw him display any sign of affection for his wife when he kissed her at the deathbed of their ten-year-old son, Ben.

One thing he clearly did remember from his childhood, however, was a young slave woman named Jenny, who had taken care of him in his sickly infancy and may have saved him once from drowning in Bear Creek. It was from her that he heard, among many other things, the ghost story of the "Golden Arm," which in years to come he would make famous by retelling it from the lecture platform, and she, more than his fierce, energetic mother who was continually busy coming to the rescue of the poor and oppressed of Hannibal, not to mention maltreated horses and abandoned cats, seems to have been the one who had the day-to-day, hands-on care of the Clemens children. On one occasion Jenny evidently stepped out of line somehow, and when Mrs. Clemens' attempt at punishing her failed, she had to call on her husband, who tied the girl's wrists together with a rein and lashed her across the shoulders with a cowhide whip. A few years later, when as usual he needed money, he sold her to a man who was notorious for his cruelty to the slaves he traded in and not long afterwards sold her down the river, never to be seen by the Clemens family again.

Looking back at the Hannibal of his boyhood, Sam remembered it as "the white town drowsing in the sunshine of a summer morning . . . the great Mississippi, the magnificent Mississippi, rolling its mile-wide tide along; . . . the dense forest away on the other side." It was justly proud of its scenery. Circled by bluffs, with Holliday's Hill on the north, Lovers' Leap on the south, the dazzling river was its highway to the outside world, with rafts drifting by downstream and the majestically ornate steamboats plying their way in both directions, their long, gilded saloons resplendent with oil paintings and crystal chandeliers, and black servants in white aprons to serve refreshments to the pilots on watch in the glass-enclosed pilot house. Hannibal ranked itself as second only to the metropolis of St. Louis, just a hundred miles away, and its population ranged from slaves and vagrants of one kind or another, through blue collar workers, tradesmen, and on up to the professional men of the community, who were its aristocracy and looked it from their tall hats, ruffled shirtfronts, swallowtail coats, and the stately brick or frame houses they lived in behind colonnaded, Greek revival façades.

But for the boy who grew up to become Mark Twain, the morning sunshine cast a menacing shadow. When he was seven, he played hooky from school one day and to postpone the inevitable thrashing climbed through the window of his father's office to spend the night there. Little by little as the moonlight advanced across the floor, he became aware first of the hand, then the naked arm, then the ashen face of a corpse, "the eyes fixed and glassy in death" as he described it later. It was the body of a murdered farmer that had been brought to Judge Clemens' office to await the undertaker the next day, and the boy never forgot it. Two years later, for the first of a number of times, he saw a murder actually take place and never forgot that either. A neighbor of the Clemenses in a fit of drunken rage vilified a local merchant named

Owsley for being a scoundrel and thief, and when Owsley got wind of it he found the man just a step or two from the Clemens house and from the distance of about four paces, with Sam and several others looking on, fired two bullets into him. It took him half an hour or so to die, stretched out on a drugstore table with a large family Bible that someone had idiotically spread open on his bleeding chest, and Sam watched it rise and fall in time to the man's labored breathing. As he wrote in his autobiography, "In my nightmares I gasped and struggled for breath under the crush of that vast book for many a night."

There were other deaths too in that drowsing white town. A childhood friend known as Dutchy drowned as the result of a game to see who could stay underwater longest in a creek that some local coopers used for soaking willow poles to make them pliant enough for hoops, and when after a long time he had not resurfaced, Sam was the one who dived down to find his lifeless body entangled in them. It was not just that memory that he carried with him the rest of his days, but also the realization that if he had not been one of the ones to egg the boy on, he might very well have been still alive. When he was ten, he saw a white man kill a slave for incompetence by bashing in his head with a lump of iron ore, saw "a young California emigrant" fatally stabbed by a drinking companion and "watched the red life gush from his breast." With some friends he was wading around in a part of the river where a runaway slave was thought to have drowned when "suddenly the negro rose before them, straight and terrible, about half his length out of the water. He had gone down feet foremost, and the loosened drift had released them." Perhaps worst of all was a death that he felt personally responsible for. One winter night, at the age of seventeen, he passed the barred window of the brick town jail, where a tramp was begging for something to light his pipe with. Feeling sorry for him, he found the money somewhere to buy him a box of the not inexpensive friction matches that had recently been invented, and a few hours later, befuddled with alcohol, the tramp accidentally set his cell on fire with them. Church bells sounded the alarm, some townspeople tried unsuccessfully to break the door down with an improvised battering ram because the marshal with his key lived some distance out of town, and Sam stood among the others watching the tramp's face with the inferno behind him as he gripped the bars. "I saw that face, so situated, every night for a long time afterward," he wrote in *Life on the Mississippi*, "and I believed myself as guilty of that man's death as if I had given him the matches purposely that he might burn himself up with them."

When he shambled out onto the lecture stage in his white broadcloth suit and snowy hair, his manuscript tucked under his arm like a ruffled hen, as an eyewitness described it, and puffing one of his perpetual cigars, what the audience saw was the greatest star of the age, who for years had enchanted the world with his wit and humanity. But when he looked in the mirror, what he saw was a man haunted by guilt and remorse. Delighted as he told his daughter Clara that he was when his friend Howells started calling him "the Whited Sepulcher," it was partly the unintended bitterness of the jest that delighted him, because no one knew better than he that inside the spotless suit he was indeed "full of dead men's bones and all uncleanness." It was not just the hideous death of the tramp that he felt responsible for, but the deaths as well of some of the people closest to him.

The most shadowy of them was the death of his sister Margaret from "a bilious fever" when she was nine and he was only a few months short of four, the family having not yet moved to Hannibal from the town of Florida. He was given to sleepwalking in those days, and one night it took him to Margaret's sickroom, where he was discovered plucking at her bedclothes the way according to popular superstition invalids did when the end was near. Sure enough, three days later she did in fact die, his mother took it as clear evidence that he had second sight, and in view of his later propensity there seems good reason to suspect that in his three-year-old mind there didn't seem to be much difference between having foreseen her death and in some way or other having brought it about. If such indeed was the case, it helps explain the way he came to understand the death of his brother Ben from an unexplained illness some three years later at the age of not quite ten. Overwhelmed by her loss, Mrs. Clemens had each of the children, including seven-year-old Sam, kneel beside the body and place a hand on his cheek. Fifty years afterwards, writing about Ben in his journal, he included two cryptic phrases: "The case of memorable treachery" and "Dead Brother Ben. My treachery to him." With no further explanation offered, it is almost as if he had come to suspect that his mere touch was fatal.

In the case of his younger brother Henry, the suspicion seemed to be confirmed. Sam was working as a cub pilot on a particularly large and lavish side-wheeler named the *Pennsylvania*, and since Henry, age nineteen, was living more or less at loose ends in St.

Louis, he wangled him a job on it doing such menial tasks as measuring woodpiles and counting coal boxes with an eye to his eventually working his way up to being something like the purser. One of the pilots was a tyrannical, hot-tempered man by the name of William Brown, who for one reason or another had it in for Sam and as the result of a fierce argument between them told the captain that the boat was no longer big enough for them both. Since the captain was not immediately able to find a replacement pilot, Sam was temporarily transferred to another boat, with Henry remaining on the *Pennsylvania*. Early one morning, four of its boilers exploded, destroying the forward third of the boat including the pilot house, and a great many people were killed, passengers and crew alike, including Brown. Severely scalded, Henry was blown clear of the wreckage to die a couple of days later in a makeshift hospital in Memphis, and while he was still alive, Sam wrote the wife of their oldest brother, Orion, "Long before this reaches you, my poor Henry—my darling, my pride, my glory, my all, will have finished his blameless career, and the light of my life will have gone out in utter darkness." He has prayed God to let him die in his brother's place, he tells her, and then adds that he has also begged him "that he would pour out the fullness [*sic*] of his just wrath upon my wicked head, but have mercy, mercy, mercy upon that unoffending boy." Fourteen years later his two-year-old son, Langdon, died of diphtheria, but Sam was convinced that it was because he had taken him out for a drive in an open carriage without sufficient protection from the cold, and on the one occasion during their forty years of friendship that he ever mentioned the boy to Howells it was to say simply—as he equally well might have in the case of Dutchy, the tramp, Margaret, Ben, and Henry—"Yes, *I* killed him."

Nor were such horrors as these all that he kept hidden behind the blue-eyed, subtle smile, the puffs of cigar smoke, the glittering white suit. If he felt guilty about his extraordinary list of tragedies, he seems to have felt almost equally so about his extraordinary success. "My hated nom de plume" is the way he described his famous pseudonym to Orion, and he well knew that the leadsman's cry of "mark twain!" meant that there were only two marks—in other words only two fathoms, or twelve feet—between the hulls of the great steamboats and disaster.

With at least part of himself he hated his success because of the way it had involved him in what he saw as the corruption of his time. "The present era of incredible rottenness is not Democratic, it is not Republican, it is *national*," he wrote his brother Orion, and he was by no means alone in feeling that way. "The depravity of the business classes of our country is not less than has been supposed, but infinitely greater," is the way Walt Whitman put it, going on to describe society in general as "canker'd, crude, superstitious, and rotten," and James Russell Lowell spoke of the "Land of Broken Promises," suggesting that Lincoln's government of the people, by the people, for the people had become instead a "Kakocracy," which was conducted "for the benefit of knaves at the cost of fools." The Gilded Age was Mark Twain's term for those post–Civil War boom years when unscrupulous individualism ran unchecked in a world of wild speculation and shifting values, and in his characteristically self-flagellating way he saw its worst excesses as merely his own writ large.

Prodded from behind by memories of his father's near pauperdom and the endless failures of feckless Orion, whom he both openly deplored and was continually bankrolling, and at the same time lured forward by the spectacle of wealth and luxury that enormously attracted him, he might well be said to have spent his whole life in pursuit of money. He mined for silver. He chose to become a Mississippi River pilot not least because of the marvelous clothes they wore—the tall silk hats, the patent-leather boots, the diamond breast pins—and the ten-dollar oyster and champagne dinners he saw them feast upon when they docked in New Orleans. He invented such things as a children's game and a new kind of scrapbook with self-sticking pages. He went into the publishing business, promoting such hack jobs as *The Life of Pope Leo XIII*, which he mistakenly believed would make his fortune because every Catholic on the globe was sure to rush out and buy a copy as a religious duty. He invested thousands in such ventures as "Kaolotype," a process for making printing plates and brass stamping dyes, a German health food called Plasmon, and most notoriously the Rube Goldberg–like Paige typesetter, which was almost the ruin of him. He ran himself ragged with his international reading and lecture tours and along the way cultivated the friendship of the likes of Ulysses S. Grant, Andrew Carnegie, and, most particularly, his benefactor, Henry Huttleston Rogers, one of the pillars of the Standard Oil trust, who told a government commission, "We are not in business for our health but are out for the dollars," and whose enemies referred to him as "Hell Hound" Rogers, compared him to a shark or a rattlesnake, and spoke of his "cannibalistic money-hunger."

It was in the summer of 1876 that Twain started work on *Huckleberry Finn* at Quarry Farm, his wife's family's place in Elmira, New York, on a hilltop overlooking the Chemung River. He found the book tough going but kept at it for fear that if he didn't, the well might run permanently dry. "I like it only tolerably well, as far as I have got," he wrote Howells, "and may possibly pigeonhole or burn the MS when it is done." Generally speaking, it was a depressing period for him. An old Hannibal friend in charge of relocating the town cemetery had written him that spring to ask what to do about the graves of his father and his brother Henry, so both of those sad deaths were on his mind, very likely summoning up the others that he had on his conscience, and soon afterward his sister Pamela and their mother came for an extended visit, further slowing down the writing which he already feared was getting him nowhere. He had had his fortieth birthday only the November before and was full of gloom both about his lost youth and whatever the future held in store for him—his father had died at the age of forty-eight. "What a curious thing life is," he wrote an old friend. "We delve away, through years of hardship, wasting toil, despondency; then comes a little butterfly season of wealth, ease, & clustering honors. Presto! ... the laurels fade and fall away. Grand result of a hard-fought, successful career and a blameless life. Piles of money, tottering age, & a broken heart." In spite of everything, however, he managed to grind out the first sixteen chapters or so of his book, set it aside until 1879 or 1880, set it aside again, and then picked it up for the third and last time the summer of 1883, which proved to be as euphoric for him as the summer of 1876 had been dismal.

He had never written with such energy and enthusiasm before and was never to do so again. From after breakfast until time for dinner six days a week there at Quarry Farm, and sometimes even on Sundays, he kept at it through mid-September like a man possessed. Occasionally he would become so exhausted that he had to take to his bed for a day or two of reading and smoking, but by and large he had never in his life felt better in every way. "I'm booming these days, got health and spirits to *waste*—got an over-plus," he wrote Howells in July. "The children are booming and my health is ridiculous." And similarly, to his mother, "I haven't had such booming working-days for many years. This summer it is no more trouble for me to write than it is to lie."

He continued to work on the book that winter and finally brought it to an end in the spring of 1884, just short of eight years after he had so inauspiciously begun it. Far from thinking, as before, that he might either pigeonhole the manuscript or burn it, he wrote his English publisher, "I've just finished writing a book, and modesty compels me to say it's a rattling good one too." It was also, of course, his undoubted masterpiece, and one can only assume that much of what there was about it that gave him such joy was knowing that, contrary to the joke to his mother about lying, he had written it out of the deepest truth of who he was and in doing so had come to terms with the shadows that all his life haunted him.

Chapter 16, apparently the last one he wrote before setting the manuscript aside in 1876, ends with a disaster. Late at night—possibly by accident, possibly just for the hell of it—a steamboat plows into Huck and Jim's raft, and Huck survives only by diving down beneath the thirty-foot paddle wheel and staying under till the danger is past. By grabbing a plank from the wreckage, he manages then to make it to shore, where at a big old-fashioned double log house he is set on by a pack of dogs. Suspecting him of being one of the Shepherdsons, with whom the Grangerfords have been feuding for so long that nobody can remember what started it, Colonel Grangerford calls to him out of the window to explain who he is and what he is up to. To save himself and Jim from being found out, he tells two lies—one, that his name is George Jackson and, two, that he fell off the steamboat. Colonel Grangerford responds by saying, "Look here, if you're telling the truth you needn't be afraid—nobody'll hurt you," and the advice is as bitterly ironic as anything that this bitterly ironic book contains.

If Huck told the truth, he would be sent back to the custody of his alcoholic brute of a father and the suffocating attempts of Miss Watson to "sivilize" him, Jim would be returned to slavery, and their one chance for freedom would be shot. Colonel Grangerford to the contrary notwithstanding, Huck knows full well that if he and Jim are to make it, he is going to have to avoid truth like the plague and keep on lying with all the skill and eloquence he can muster. Part of what makes the book as savage an indictment of the human race as *Gulliver's Travels*—both of them, to add yet another irony, surviving mainly as adventure books for the young—is that *everybody* lies in it. The innocent lie in order to save their skins, and the corrupt lie in order to dupe the innocent.

When Huck says his name is George Jackson and that he fell off the steamboat, he is only getting started. Later on, in answer to the prodding of the Grangerford women, he uses it as the basis for yet another of a series of elaborate new identities that he invents during the course of the narrative. "I told them how pap and me and all the family was living on a little farm down at the bottom of Arkansaw, and my sister Mary Ann run off and got married and never was heard of no more, and Bill went to hunt them and he warn't heard of no more, and Tom and Mort died, and then there warn't nobody but just me and pap left, and he was just trimmed down to nothing, on account of his troubles; so when he died I took what there was left, because the farm didn't belong to us, and started up the river, deck passage, and fell overboard; and that was how I come to be here." In addition to being a total fabrication, his account is so poignant and persuasive that the family comes to accept him as one of their own, and he has the time of his life in their elegant, aristocratic house, the first of its kind he has ever seen, with the fancy clock on the mantelpiece that sometimes struck "a hundred and fifty before she got tuckered out," the china parrots, the books, the pictures of Washington, Highland Mary, the Signing of the Declaration, not to mention the tombstones, dead birds, mourning widows and weeping willows done in crayon by the late Emmeline Grangerford, of whom he says in one of the novel's richest comic passages, "Everybody was sorry she died . . . but I reckoned that with her disposition she was having a better time in the graveyard."

Not wanting to do anything that might rock the boat and bring his idyll to an end, he lies again to lovely twenty-year-old Sophia Grangerford by saying that he is unable to read the handwritten note that he has unwittingly delivered to her from a son of the hated Shepherdsons, and in general he is successful at avoiding anything that might blow his cover by drawing increased attention to him until circumstances beyond his control finally overwhelm him. The clandestine note appoints the hour when the young lovers are to run off together, and as soon as it is discovered, the feud heats up and all hell breaks loose. Slim, elegant Colonel Grangerford is killed together with two of his older sons, and then Huck's particular friend, Buck, and a cousin are shot before his eyes. "It made me so sick I most fell out of the tree," he says. "I ain't a-going to tell *all* that happened—it would make me sick again," but in spite of himself he tells enough. "When I got down out of the tree I crept along down the river-bank a piece, and found the two bodies laying in the edge of the water, and tugged at them till I got them ashore; then I covered up their faces, and got away as quick as I could. I cried a little when I was covering up Buck's face, for he was mighty good to me." It is shortly afterwards that he comes upon Jim, who has managed to repair the smashed raft enough for them to continue their escape on it, and at the sound of his voice—"nothing ever sounded so good before"—they fall into each other's arms. Once they have drifted downstream some two miles, Jim cooks them some pork and cabbage, and Huck comments, "We said there warn't no home like a raft, after all. Other places do seem so cramped up and smothery, but a raft don't. You feel mighty free and easy and comfortable on a raft." In other words, he is George Jackson no longer, but once again Huck Finn, the truth of whom—which he has had to lie to keep safe—is his tears over Buck, the emotion that the sound of Jim's voice stirs in him, and his joy at rediscovering the raft that will carry them both to the freedom he hungers for above all else.

As far as Huck is concerned, the freedom he hungers for is mainly freedom from Pap's brutality, on the one hand, and the well-intentioned but dismally constraining solicitudes of Miss Watson and the Widow Douglas, on the other. To the degree that he has a plan at all other than simply to cut loose, it is to let the raft drift with the current as far south as Cairo, where they will sell it and with the proceeds take a steamboat up the Ohio to the nonslavery states in the north, where Jim will at last be free. But in Mark Twain's mind, Huck was cutting loose from more than just that.

"I have been reading the morning paper," he wrote Howells in 1899. "I do it every morning—well knowing that I shall find in it the usual depravities and basenesses & hypocrisies & cruelties that make up Civilization, and cause me to put in the rest of the day pleading for the damnation of the human race," which of course included his own damnation, as he was always the first to proclaim. Just as he felt that he himself had been corrupted by that civilization, he feared for what it might ultimately do also to this child of his fancy, whom he so clearly loved in the same way that, despite his characteristic self-loathing, he still seems to have loved the child that he liked to believe Sam Clemens had been once upon a time in Hannibal. Thus in his mind it was not just the drunken vagrant and the two pious sisters that Huck needed to cut loose from, but the Gilded Age itself.

"Big and scary, with a long row of wide-open furnace doors shining like red-hot teeth and her monstrous bows and guards hanging right over us" is the way the steamboat that all but destroyed the two fugitives is described, and the hellish allusions suggest that it was more than just a steamboat that Mark Twain and presumably Huck as well had in mind. Although nowhere in his writings does he ever allude to it directly—the sacrosanctness for him of not just the great Mississippi as he idealized it, but everything associated with it seems to have silenced him—his experience as a pilot had made him more aware than most of how the great boats were floating representations of the damned human race at its damnedest. Like the one that killed Henry Clemens, they were perpetually catching fire and blowing up not only because of their often shoddy construction from materials as combustible as much of their cargoes, but because the captains were apt to be more concerned with speed and racing their rivals than with the safety of the passengers. "Floating brothels" was one of the names they were known by, and in addition to the whores and pimps they carried gamblers, card sharks, thieves, rapists, con men, and assorted rowdies and predators, not to mention the inevitable collection of slaves being hauled by their masters from one place of servitude to another like luggage. It was the captain alone who was responsible for maintaining law and order, and at his say-so, after appearing before a kangaroo court composed of fellow passengers, miscreants could be flogged, made to run the gauntlet, or tossed overboard to fend for themselves in the wilderness. Although a boy living in a river town like Hannibal would have been certainly aware of all this, Twain does not have Huck say anything to make us think he was, and yet at the same time there is the suggestion in the infernal imagery he uses—the red-hot teeth and monstrous bows—that in a general way he intuits the corruption not only of the boat that was almost the end of him and others like it, but of the society that produced them.

At the end of *Tom Sawyer,* Tom and Huck are given six thousand dollars apiece from the robbers' hoard, and one of the first things Huck does in the sequel is to try to persuade Judge Thatcher to take it off his hands both because it is a continual cause of trouble with his father, who is always after him for it, and also because, as he says, "I don't want to spend it. I don't want it at all," as if he senses that money and the power it has to earn more money still and thus attract more people to try getting it out of him, is somehow at the root of everything he wants to be free of. It is contrary to all expectations for him not to want the six thousand dollars and, more remarkable still, he eventually decides that although beatings from Pap are an almost daily occurrence he also does not want to return to the Widow Douglas because in spite of all the creature comforts he enjoys in her care, she represents to him no less a threat to his freedom and integrity than the money and the steamboat with its red-hot teeth. It is not until in a fit of delirium tremens Pap takes him for the angel of death and comes at him with a knife that he realizes it is not just his freedom now that is being threatened but his life itself, and in order to save it he fakes his own death.

It is the acting out of one of the most intricate of all his lies, and he goes about it with the same thoroughness and ingenuity that he later put into his many false identities, including those of George Jackson, Sarah Williams, George Peters, and others that he invents along the way. He shoots a wild hog and scatters its blood all over the place including the blade of an axe. For good measure he also pulls out some of his own hair and adds that as well. He drags a sack of rocks down to the river and throws it in to make it look as though that was how his body was disposed of. He rips a hole in a bag of meal to leave a trail and carries it off in another direction so people will think it was the route the murderer took making away with his loot. After accomplishing all that and narrowly escaping Pap, who by this time has returned, he floats off into the night lying in the bottom of his canoe so no one will see him. "I laid there and had a good rest and a smoke out of my pipe, looking away into the sky; not a cloud in it. The sky looks ever so deep when you lay down on your back in the moonshine; I never knowed it before," he says, nor was it only the fathomless sky that was new to him. It was also the realization that having gotten rid once and for all of his money, of the Widow Douglas and Miss Watson, of the fancy clothes they made him wear and the school they made him wear them to, of the nightmare brutalizations of his father, and now having gone so far as to have in effect gotten rid even of the boy named Huckleberry Finn himself, he is at last reduced—like Father Hopkins bathing in that "sweetest, freshest, shadowiest" woodland pool and King Lear stripped of his "lend-ings" on the heath—to his bare and essential humanness. As he lies there smoking his pipe in the moonlight, the suggestion is that he has reached something not unlike the peace that passes all under-standing.

Later on when he has teamed up with Jim and they are on their way downstream, Huck says, "We was always naked, day and night, whenever the mosquitoes would let us." Twain makes little of it, never mentioning it again, nor have I ever seen it especially noted by anybody else writing on the subject, but it seems to me a remarkable and telling part of what the book is saying. The two of them are no longer a man and a boy, a black and a white, an illiterate and a literate, a slave and a master. Bare as birth—or rebirth—they are simply two members of the human race who are at least for the time being beyond the reach of damnation. "Thou art the thing itself," Lear says to Edgar in his nakedness, as he might equally well have said it here. "Unaccommodated man is no more but such a poor, bare, forked animal as thou art." No more perhaps, but, in the dehumanized and dehumanizing world that both *King Lear* and *Huckleberry Finn* portray, also no less.

In feigning death Huck takes a new hold on his life; in renouncing his share of the robbers' treasure he stumbles on the treasure of the night sky; without a stitch on him he braves the elements more bravely than ever; and with his marvelous talent for mendacity he saves not only his own neck but in the process, over and over again, Jim's as well. He does not do so as a self-conscious work of charity such as he has learned about from religiously inclined slave owners or in response to the fiery exhortations of preachers like the one he heard at the Parkville camp meeting. On the contrary, he does it fully believing that, in helping his friend escape, he is in effect robbing Miss Watson of her rightful property and thus doing the work of the devil. The conscience that has been formed in him by the church-going citizenry of Hannibal tells him that he should turn Jim in, and when he finally resolves to follow its dictates, he feels "easy and happy and light as a feather." As he starts paddling away to do so, Jim, thinking that he is simply heading for shore to see if they have reached the gateway to freedom at Cairo yet, cries out, "Dah you goes, de ole true Huck; de on'y white genlman dat ever kep' his promise to ole Jim," and Huck is devastated. When two armed men shortly appear in a skiff looking for runaway slaves, he tells them that the man on the raft is not one of them, but instead his smallpox-infected father, which sends them packing, as of course Huck is shrewd enough in the ways of the world to know it will. What "de ole true Huck" is true to, needless to say, is no creed or ethic, but the truth of his own heart, and by following its bidding, he little by little comes aware of the truth of Jim's too.

Mark Twain's sister-in-law, Susan Crane, had a study built for him at Quarry Farm some hundred yards up the hill from the main house, and it was there that, at various periods over the years, he wrote the bulk of *Huckleberry Finn*. Vaguely resembling a pilot house, it consisted of a smallish, octagonal room with six large windows, one cut through the chimney over the mantelpiece, which gave a spectacular view of "leagues of valley and city and retreating ranges of distant blue hills," as he described it to his Congregational minister friend Joe Twichell. "The loveliest study you ever saw." He would start work directly after breakfast and keep at it, usually skipping lunch, until about five or so in the afternoon, when he would rejoin his family and later on read them what he had produced that day. It is hard to imagine that he read any of it with more feeling or with more of himself in it than the parts describing how Huck gradually comes to understand who and what Jim truly is. In an often quoted passage in which he lies to Aunt Sally Phelps about a steamboat accident that actually never took place, she asks him, "Good gracious! anybody hurt?" to which his classic reply is "No'm. Killed a nigger," and nothing in the novel is more touching or convincing than the way, in spite of himself and of everything he has been brought up to believe, he comes to another view.

An early stage along the way takes place when for the sheer dev-iltry of it Huck pretends to his friend that they had never gotten separated in the fog—he in the canoe and Jim on the raft—and that Jim must have simply dreamed the whole thing. Jim had been beside himself with worry and when he discovers that Huck has been simply playing a trick on him, he make no bones about how he feels. "When I got all wore out wid work, en wid de callin' for you, en went to sleep," he says, "my heart wuz mos' broke bekase you wuz los', en I didn' k'yer no' mo' what become er me en de raf'. . . . En all you wuz thinkin' 'bout was how you could make a fool uv ole Jim wid a lie." Huck is overwhelmed with shame, and as he describes it, "It was fifteen minutes before I could work myself up to go and humble myself to a nigger; but I done it, and I warn't even sorry about it afterward, neither." More importantly, from that time on, he says, he "didn't do him no more mean tricks," as the journey down the river becomes for him a search for freedom not just from everything that threatens from without, but also from the shadows within.

It is considerably later in the narrative that he is awakened on the raft one night by the sound of Jim's weeping and realizes that "though it don't seem natural," it is because he is as homesick for his wife and children as a white man would be. When Huck asks about them, Jim replies with the account of how one day when his four-year-old daughter 'Lizabeth failed to shut the door when he asked her to, he "fetch' her a slap side de head dat sont her a-sprawlin'" and only afterwards discovered that, unknown to him, she was deaf and dumb from scarlet fever. Later on when the scoundrelly Duke and Dauphin paint him blue and dress him up as

King Lear to keep him from being recognized as a runaway, one wonders if it can possibly have been the parallel between the old king's remorse over Cordelia and Jim's over 'Lizabeth that led Twain, consciously or otherwise, to pick that one costume in particular. Be that as it may, Jim's lament comes from such a deep place within him and comes with such raw power that Huck lets it stand without comment. "De Lord God Amighty fogive po' ole Jim, kaze he never gwyne to fogive hisself as long's he live," he says, and in the manuscript Twain has heavily underlined the words and written in the margin, "This expression shall not be changed." When he read it out loud in the living room at Quarry Farm, no one present can have been more moved than he was—not even Huck—or can have known better what it meant to cry out of the depths to be forgiven the unforgivable.

In one of the final chapters, still troubled by his conscience about helping a slave escape, Huck gets down on his knees and tries to pray to be able to give up his sin, but the words will not come out, and in his heart he knows that it is because if giving up his sin means betraying Jim, he has no real intention of doing it and "You can't pray a lie," as the chapter is entitled. Consequently, he grits his teeth and writes a note to Miss Watson telling her exactly where and how Jim is to be found and recaptured, and because the passage that follows is central not only to Huck's inward journey but also to the novel as a whole, it needs to be given in full.

I felt good and all washed clean of sin for the first time I had never felt so in my life, and I knowed I could pray now. But I didn't do it straight off, but laid the paper down and set there thinking—thinking how good it was all this happened so, and how near I come to being lost and going to hell. And went on thinking. And got to thinking over our trip down the river; and I see Jim before me all the time: in the day and in the night-time, sometimes moonlight, sometimes storms, and we a-floating along, talking and singing and laughing. But somehow I couldn't seem to strike no places to harden me against him, but only the other kind. I'd see him standing my watch on top of his'n, 'stead of callin' me, so I could go on sleeping; and see him how glad he was when I come back out of the fog; and when I come to him again in the swamp, up there where the feud was; and such-like times; and would always call me honey, and pet me, and do everything he could think of for me, and how good he always was; and at last I struck the time I saved him by telling the men we had smallpox aboard, and he was so grateful, and said I was the best friend old Jim ever had in the world, and the *only* one he's got now; and then I happened to look around and see that paper.

It was a close place. I took it up, and held it in my hand. I was a-trembling, because I'd got to decide, forever, betwixt two things, and I knowed it. I studied a minute, sort of holding my breath, and then says to myself:

"All right, then, I'll *go* to hell"—and tore it up.

It is easy to understand the almost manic excitement with which Mark Twain wrote his last chapters that golden summer of 1883. He had found by then not only Huckleberry Finn's true voice, but also his own, and he knew it. Every word fell into the right place and was the right word. Every feeling that he conveyed was unforced, convincing, authentic, and his characters had acquired such all but independent life that he could devote his artistry to just listening to them with fascination and letting them go their own ways. Despite his horror at the condition of the human race, including himself, he had discovered in the heart of his hero a measure of honesty, unsentimental compassion, and genuine goodness that he could affirm without qualification. It is not only Jim that Huck takes pity on, but even the two murderers who face drowning on the wreck of the *Walter Scott*—"I says to myself, there ain't no telling but I might come to be a murderer myself yet, and then how would I like it?"—and with one of his ingenious whoppers he arranges to have them rescued before the boat breaks up and sinks. The Duke and the Dauphin, those unparalleled masters of the con game and the double cross, have taken advantage of him in every imaginable way and connived to sell Jim back into slavery for a mere forty dollars in return for all his weeks of waiting on them hand and foot, but after unsuccessfully trying to warn them of what is coming, he happens upon them one day in tar and feathers being ridden out of town on a rail, as they richly deserve, to the music of catcalls, banging tin pans, and blowing horns, and his heart goes out to them too. "Well, it made me sick to see it," he says, "and I was sorry for them poor pitiful rascals, it seems like I couldn't ever feel any hardness against them any more in the world."

There is hope for the world in hearts like Huck's and Jim's and here and there a few others. Mary Jane Wilks buries her face in her hands and weeps real tears at the thought of her dead uncle's slaves being sold separately, the mother up the river to Memphis, the sons down the river to New Orleans; and when Jim is being held under lock and key at the Phelps plantation, Uncle Silas and Aunt Sally keep coming in to pray with him and make sure he has plenty to eat; and in the final chapter, we learn from Tom Sawyer that Miss Watson felt such remorse at having considered selling Jim down south that, shortly before her death two months earlier, she set him free in her will.

But all of these are little more than glimmers in a world whose essential darkness Mark Twain was no more able to minimize than he could the darkness within himself. Almost everyone Huck and Jim run into on their journey is motivated by nothing so much as greed and self-interest. The citizens of Parkville are stirred to a religious frenzy, sobbing and flinging themselves about as they surge forward in answer to the camp-meeting preacher's altar call—"come, black with sin! . . . come, sick and sore! . . . come, pore and needy, sunk in shame!"—but they are indistinguishable from the people a few miles farther down the river in Arkansas who amuse themselves by tormenting nursing sows, setting fire to turpentine-drenched dogs or tying tin pans to their tails and watching them run themselves to death, and it is in the same town that Huck witnesses a very similar version of the murder that as a boy in Hannibal Mark Twain himself had seen committed by the man named Owsley only a few steps from the Clemens house.

With his alcoholic ranting and buffoonery, one Boggs—"the best-naturedest old fool in Arkansaw, never hurt nobody drunk or sober"—antagonizes Colonel Sherburn—"proud-looking . . . best dressed man in that town"—to the point where the Colonel tells him that unless he stops vilifying him by one o'clock, it will be the worse for him. When Boggs disregards the warning, Sherburn with chilling calm and precision shoots him in the chest twice with his double-barreled pistol in full view of Boggs' sixteen-year-old daughter, who has come to try to drag her father home, and the townspeople push and shove their way into the drugstore to watch him die, one of them reenacting the crime so successfully, using his cane for the gun, that "as much as a dozen people got out their bottles and treated him."

In its way almost more chilling is the famous passage in which, when the mob turns up at his house later to lynch him, the Colonel confronts them from the roof of his front porch, at first not saying a word but just standing there, calm and deliberate, as he looks down on them with his pistol in his hand until they drop their eyes and fall silent. "Because you're brave enough to tar and feather poor friendless cast-out women that come along here, did that make you think you had grit enough to lay your hands on a *man?* Why, a *man's* safe in the hands of ten thousand of your kind— as long as it's daytime and you're not behind him." By the time he finishes, mocking them as cowards and half-men—"If any real lynching's going to be done it will be done in the dark, Southern fashion"—they are so abashed that they break ranks and go tearing off in defeat. As Huck says on another occasion, "It was enough to make a body ashamed of the human race."

To be ashamed of the human race is to be as a stranger in its midst, and maybe that is part at least of why Huck speaks so often of loneliness, starting with the first time we ever see him when he is still living at the Widow Douglas' with his adventures not yet begun. He chafes at the new clothes she makes him wear and at the school he has to wear them to and at not being allowed to smoke. He is depressed by having to get to meals on the dot of time and then having to wait for her to "tuck down her head and grumble a little over the victuals" before being allowed to start eating. He loses interest in the Bible when he learns that Moses has been dead for years, and when Miss Watson tells him he must learn to behave himself so he will go to heaven, his response is "I couldn't see no advantage in going where she was going, so I made up my mind I wouldn't try for it." In other words, if the lynch mob and their like made him feel ashamed of the human race, the respectability of the widow and Miss Watson made him feel ashamed of himself, and in both cases he was left with a sense of estrangement and isolation. But his deepest loneliness comes from somewhere else, and we catch a glimpse of it at the very start of the novel when, after everybody else has retired for the night, he goes up to his bedroom, lights a candle, and sits in a chair at the window.

The rustling leaves, the owl's call, the crying out of a dog, everything he hears speaks to him of sadness and death. The wind is trying to whisper something to him that he can't make out, and there is a sound in the woods "that a ghost makes when it wants to tell about something that's on its mind and can't make itself understood, and so can't rest easy in its grave, and has to go about that way every night grieving."

Such is the darkness that comes to him through the window, and it is no greater than the darkness that comes from within. "I felt so lonesome," he says, "I most wished I was dead," and one is reminded both of Mark Twain's "from the cradle up I have been like the rest of the race—never quite sane in the night," and of Gerard Manley Hopkins' "I cast for comfort I can no more get / By groping round my comfortless, than blind / Eyes in their dark can day." Farther along in the novel, Twain speaks of even the great river itself as lonesome with no boats in sight for sometimes as much as an hour at a time but "just solid lonesomeness." And farther along still, at the Phelpses' plantation, the dim dronings of bugs and flies in the air sound so lonesome to him that he feels "like everybody's dead and gone" and wishes "*he* was dead too, and done with it all," a feeling that is confirmed by the faint hum of a spinning wheel, which leads him to say it again: "I knowed for certain I wished I was dead—for that *is* the lonesomest sound in the whole world." He is lonesome because nothing Widow Douglas and Miss Watson ever said gave him a faith to draw comfort from. He is lonesome because he is alone in the night and there is no one, not even Tom Sawyer, who can save him from finally being swallowed up by it. He is lonesome because he knows that someday he will die.

But in the meantime he will get by, and he knows it. No less than Jim, he has made his escape and become owner of himself in a new way. Pap is dead and, no less liberatingly, so is Miss Watson. The Duke and the Dauphin have vanished in a flurry of tar and feathers to work their ineffable scams elsewhere. Even the conscience that told him he would go to hell for helping Jim no longer has a hold on him because, after successfully defying it, he from that time on "never thought no more about reforming." More maybe than anything else, in addition to friends like Tom Sawyer, he has Jim and whatever it was in himself that made it worth risking even damnation to save him, and with it he has the memory of whatever it was in Jim that made him stand watches for him on the raft at night and call him Honey and weep tears of rejoicing when he found him again after they had become separated in the fog.

The lonesomeness and the dark are always there, but so is the river—"I reckon I got to light out for the territory ahead of the rest" he says in his last sentence—and wherever the mighty current takes him there will be new adventures even more marvelous than Tom Sawyer's because, unlike Tom, in the fullest sense of the phrase, Huckleberry Finn has his heart in them.

As far as Mark Twain's own heart is concerned, it would not be too much to say that on August 18, 1896, just twelve years after finishing his masterpiece, it was broken in such a way that it was never to heal. Accompanied by his wife, Livy, and their youngest daughter, Clara, he was on an around-the-world lecture tour whose purpose was to make him enough money to pay back dollar for dollar all the debts he was left with when his publishing company failed and at his friend Henry Rogers' advice he declared bankruptcy. Clara and Livy, on their way back to America, got the news from the ship's captain. Mark Twain, staying on in a house they had rented in England, learned of it through a cable sent by Livy's brother, Charles Langdon. Susie Clemens, the oldest of his three daughters, had died of spinal meningitis in the family home in Hartford. She was twenty-four-years old, and as an old man, in his posthumously published autobiography, he described the effect of her death on him in one of the richest of his images.

It is one of the mysteries of our nature that a man, all unprepared, can receive a thunder-stroke like that and live. There is but one reasonable explanation of it. The intellect is stunned by the shock and but gropingly gathers the meaning of the words. The power to realize their full import is mercifully wanting. The mind has a dumb sense of vast loss—that is all. It will take mind and memory months, and possibly years, to gather together the details and thus learn and know the whole extent of the loss. A man's house burns down. The smoking wreckage represents only a ruined home that was dear through years of use and pleasant associations. By and by, as the days and weeks go on, first he misses this, then that, then the other thing. And when he casts about for it he finds that it was in that house. Always it is an *essential*—there was but one of its kind. It cannot be replaced. It was in that house. It is irrevocably lost. He did not realize that it was an essential when he had it; he only discovers it now when he finds himself balked, hampered, by its absence. It will be years before the tale of lost essentials is complete, and not till then can he truly know the magnitude of the disaster.

As in so many earlier cases, he felt personally responsible for the tragedy, and his reasoning, such as it was, is not hard to follow. If his folly and greed had not led him into bankruptcy, he would not have had to go barreling around the world to recoup his losses—"I am demeaning myself," he wrote, adding, with the grotesque shenanigans of the Duke and Dauphin possibly in the back of his

mind, "I am allowing myself to be a mere buffoon. It's ghastly"—
and if he had not done that, both he and, more importantly, Livy
would have been there in Hartford when Susie was taken sick, and
if that had been the case, with her own mother to look after her,
she would somehow have survived. Unable to get back to Elmira
in time for the funeral, he wrote Livy, "She died in our own
house—not in another's; died where every little thing was familiar
and beloved; died where she had spent all her life till my crimes
made her a pauper and an exile." In other words, in his own mind
he had killed her as surely as he had killed her brother, Langdon,
many years before by taking him on that fateful carriage ride, and
he and Livy never recovered from the devastation of the blow.

To make his sense of guilt even more overpowering, he believed
that it was thanks to him that Livy no longer had her religious faith
to fall back on, and in this case he was probably right. Although Joe
Twichell remained a great friend to the end, Mark Twain had long
since stopped attending his church, and in time Livy did too,
explaining her decision by saying, "Well, if you are lost, I want to
be lost with you." After Susie's death, he told her, "Livy, if it comforts you to lean on the Christian faith, do so," and her reply, using
the name she always called him by, was "I can't, Youth. I haven't
any." As his friend and biographer Albert Bigelow Paine wrote,
"The thought that he had destroyed her illusion, without affording
a compensating solace, was one that would come back to him,
now and then, all his days." All in all, what with Livy's death in
1904, followed by their daughter Jean's on Christmas Eve in
1909, the darkness and the lonesomeness became more than the
Huck Finn in him could handle, and in his last writings, too full

of bitterness, despair, and near madness to be published until after his death, he resorted to a kind of confused, vindictive nihilism.

In *The Mysterious Stranger,* Satan says, "*Nothing* exists," and then, "Strange, indeed, that you should not have suspected that your universe and its contents were only dreams, visions, fiction! Strange, because they are so frankly and hysterically insane—like all dreams. . . . There is no God, no universe, no human race, no earthly life, no heaven, no hell. It is all a dream—a grotesque and foolish dream. Nothing exists but you. And you are but a *thought*— a vagrant thought, a homeless thought, wandering forlorn among the empty eternities!" And against all this, he wrote elsewhere, the human race has only "one really effective weapon—laughter." But it was a far cry from the laughter of *Huckleberry Finn,* with Huck and Jim's unforgettable discussion of "King Sollermun" and his "'bout five million chillen runnin' roun' de house," and the under-taker at Peter Wilks' funeral who "was the glidingest, stealthiest man I ever see; and there warn't no more smile to him than there is to a ham," and the way one of the black men they meet on their travels "smiled around graduly over his face, like when you heave a brickbat in a mud-puddle."

Nevertheless the old superstar apparently kept on going to the end. He would lie in his ornately carved Florentine bed in his room at Stormfield, where, as a child, a friend of mine was once taken by his father on some errand only to be scared half out of his wits by an ancient, snowy-haired apparition almost lost to view in clouds of cigar smoke; and it was often from there that he would dictate the reminiscences that Paine said "bore only an atmospheric relation to history." When burglars broke in and stole the family silver, he posted a message to them on the front door that read in part: "There is nothing but plated ware in this house, now and henceforth. You will find it in the brass thing in the dining-room over in the corner by the basket of kittens. If you want the basket, put the kittens in the brass thing." In Bermuda and elsewhere, he made friends with a number of pretty little girls whom he called his "Angel fish" and wrote letters to them full of foolishness and wit. When Paine photographed him in a series of seven ruminative poses sitting white-suited in a rocking chair on the porch of the Dublin, New Hampshire, house that he rented the summer of 1906 after Livy's death, Twain scrawled in descriptions of what he was ruminating about in each : (1) "Shall I learn to be good?" (2) "There do seem to be many diffi. . . , " (3) "and yet if I should *really* try," (4) "and just put my *heart* in it," until the seventh and final one, which reads, "Oh, never mind. I reckon I'm good enough just as I am." And above all, he talked, and talked, and talked—endlessly, disarmingly, fascinatingly, so that after having dinner with him in 1907 William James described him in a letter to his brother Henry with the words, "Poor man, only good for monologue, in his old age, or for dialogue at best, but he's a dear little genius all the same."

William's pity is touching in a way and certainly understandable, but to a degree it was also misplaced. With all those monologues, the dear little genius was doing quite brilliantly at not being swamped by lonesomeness and at piloting a course around both the darkness of the past and the darkness that he knew awaited him not much farther downstream.

PART 3

G. K. CHESTERTON:
THE MAN WHO NEVER
STOPPED TALKING

G K. Chesterton was given to doing something odd with the match whenever he lit a cigar—he smoked as prodigiously as he drank wine, ate, talked, above all wrote and according to a friend what he was up to was making the sign of the cross, as he also did on the door whenever he entered a room. But he did so many other odd things that the chances are nobody much noticed. He was continually losing his way, sometimes within a stone's throw of his own house—or even *in* his own house, he claimed— forgetting things, losing track of what time or even what day it was, and drawing pictures on blotters, napkins, walls, virtually any surface that presented itself. He would take a cab halfway up a street, keep it waiting for an hour or so, and then take it back the other half. Busy as his schedule was, he rarely knew where he was supposed to be at any given hour, and his sister-in-law remembered drinking burgundy with him in a wine shop in Fleet Street when he suddenly announced that in an hour or so he was supposed to be giving a lecture in Buckinghamshire. The story is also told of how he once kept an appointment with his publisher during the course of which he handed over a note of apology for not being able to keep it, and his writing habits were equally memorable. An endless torrent of articles, reviews, essays, and poems tumbled from his pen, and often he composed them on the run—

in a tea room, on top of a double-decker bus, standing in the door-way of a shop, or leaning against a wall scribbling in pencil in a penny exercise book or sometimes just on his cuff. He read as continuously as he wrote, and his friend Father John O'Connor, the prototype for Father Brown, the most famous of his fictional characters, said that when he finished with a book, it looked as though "It had gone through every indignity a book may suffer and live. He turned it inside out, dog-eared it, penciled it, sat on it, took it to bed and rolled on it, and got up again and spilled tea on it." His enemy, the militant atheist Robert Blatchford, contemptuously maintained that it was all just a pose—"He played a part and dressed for a part"—but, if so, he played it for so long that he ended by becoming it. On the other hand, to read about his early years is to see that he began acting not quite like anybody else in the world long before it can have occurred to him that he was doing anything but simply being himself.

He was in his twenties when he started carrying a sword-stick whose blade sometimes slipped out and went clattering to the pavement as he moved about the London streets. His younger brother, Cecil, maintained that it was not an affectation but that he carried it because, in his romantic imagination, he always dreamed of being caught up in some amazing adventure in which he would need it for defending himself. He had been thin as a boy, but by then he had become a husky young man, six feet two, handsome, with wavy, chestnut-colored hair, delicate hands, and unusually small feet, which seemed inadequate to the task of giving him the solid base he needed, especially as he began to put on more and more weight. Like his colleagues at the publishing firm of Fisher

Unwin, he went to work in a black frock coat and tall silk hat, but he dressed so sloppily—the coat in need of brushing, the tie askew, one wing of his stiff collar as likely as not flapping free of its stud, and the hat out of shape—that finally Frances Blogg, the young woman he was soon to marry, decided she must take him in hand.

Since he always looked grotesque in the conventional clothes that he never took proper care of, she reasoned that it would be better for him to look picturesque instead and persuaded him to exchange the frock coat for a flowing cape and his battered topper for a slouch hat with a wide brim, which, together with his pince-nez and blond moustache, transformed him into what he described as "that Falstaffian figure in a brigand's hat and cloak" that became his public image for the rest of his days. Although as the years went by he got bigger and bigger until he eventually reached something like three hundred pounds or more, his voice, which hadn't changed until he was almost out of school, remained high-pitched—"the mouse that came forth from the mountain" he called it—and according to the novelist Frank Swinnerton his speech was always "prefaced and accompanied by a curious sort of humming, such as one may hear when glee singers give each other the note before starting to sing." It was a voice he used more than most because in the midst of his incessant writing, he somehow managed to spend more time on the lecture circuit than even Mark Twain—whom Chesterton was one of a group of English authors to send a congratulatory cable on the occasion of his seventieth birthday in 1905—and his extraordinary figure on the platform was no less familiar and unmistakable. According to a journalist who interviewed him at the Biltmore Hotel on a visit to New York, when an American woman said to him, "Everyone seems to know you, Mr. Chesterton," his "mournful" answer was, "Yes, and if they don't, they ask."

By all accounts his childhood was an exceptionally happy one, and the best pages of his posthumously published autobiography are the ones describing it.

I regret that I have no savage and gloomy father to offer to the public gaze as the true cause of all my tragic heritage, no pale-faced and partially poisoned mother whose suicidal instincts have cursed me with the temptations of the artistic tempera-ment. I regret that there was nothing in the range of our fam-ily much more racy than a remote and mildly impecunious uncle; and that I cannot do my duty as a true modern, by cursing everybody who made me whatever I am. I am not clear about what that is; but I am pretty sure that most of it is my own fault. And I am compelled to confess that I look back to that landscape of my first days with a pleasure that should doubtless be reserved for the Utopias of the Futurist.

Far from being savage and gloomy, his father, Edward Chesterton, "might have reminded people of Mr. Pickwick except that he was always bearded and never bald," but he was also terrified of sick-ness and death—a trait he passed along to his son—and when the first child, Beatrice, died at the age of eight while Chesterton was still little more than an infant, he is said to have turned her portrait to the wall and begged his wife never to mention her name again in his presence so that from that time on it was as if she had never existed. Otherwise he was apparently in the richest sense Pickwickian and, after retiring early from the family real estate business in Kensington because he was convinced that he had a bad heart, seems to have spent the rest of his life more or less staying at home and enjoying himself with his countless hobbies—painting, modeling in plastiscene, coloring magic lantern slides, learning how to use a camera, and at one point, when telephones were just starting to appear, turning out one of his own with which he could communicate from the topmost story of the house to the far end of the garden. Most magical of all, his son wrote, was a toy theater that he not only made with his fretsaw but also served as scene designer and scene painter, writing playlets for it that were performed by actors and actresses, also of his own manufacture, only a few inches high. According to Chesterton the earliest memory he had was of looking through the proscenium and seeing one of these little figures standing on a bridge with a golden crown on his head and in his hand an enormous golden key. As his friend and biographer Maisie Ward wrote, "his father was all through his childhood a man with a golden key who admitted him into a world of wonders."

His mother was another kettle of fish altogether, and although he evidently always spoke of her with affection, he never described her in the autobiography and scarcely so much as mentioned her. Friends of Chesterton who knew her all agreed that she was immensely kind and respectful to them—always calling them by their last names even as little boys—but at the same time was rather terrifying to look at with her "clothes thrown on anyhow, and blackened and protruding teeth which gave her a witchlike appearance." Though physically small and fragile, she is reported to have been bursting with energy, a witty conversationalist devoted both to the husband she dominated and the two sons she adored, and an enthusiastic hostess who liked nothing more than serving gargantuan meals to a houseful of guests.

Chesterton was a slow starter—he was almost three before he started to talk much and didn't learn to read until he was eight—but he was always drawing pictures, which his father carefully put away with the date on each, and he loved fairy tales, particularly George MacDonald's *The Princess and the Goblins*, which, he said, made "a difference to my whole existence ... helped me to see things in a different way from the start." In the large house where the Princess was brought up there was a mysterious old fairy godmother of a woman who lived in a hidden room upstairs with a group of malevolent goblins in caverns down below, and Chesterton described the effect of the story upon him as making "all the ordinary staircases and doors and windows into magical things," and, more importantly still in terms of the way his life developed, as leading him to understand that "when the evil things besieging us do appear, they do not appear outside but inside."

He was thirteen years old when his parents enrolled him at the venerable school of St. Paul's, which had moved from the City to Hammersmith and was thus only a short walk from where the Chestertons lived. Milton, Pepys, and the Duke of Marlborough among others had all gone there before him, but of more immediate significance to the odd boy whose voice was not to change much before he graduated at eighteen was the fact that since it was a day school he was able to live at home and thus escape such horrors as flogging and fagging, which in those days were the common fare of the sons of English gentlemen who were packed off to boarding school. Comments from his various form masters still survive. "December 1887. Too much for me: means well by me, I believe, but has an inconceivable knack of forgetting at the shortest notice.... July 1888. Wildly inaccurate about everything.... July 1889. A great blunderer with much intelligence.... July 1891. He has a decided literary aptitude but does not trouble himself enough about school work.... July 1892. Not a quick brain, but possessed of a slowly moving tortuous imagination. Conduct always admirable." Drawing was what interested and delighted him most, but in his senior year he entered a poetry contest and won it with a poem about St. Francis Xavier, and a year or so later when his mother, concerned about the young man's future, went to consult the High Master—a gigantic man with a booming voice who may have inspired the character of Sunday in the best of all his novels—what he said to her was, "Six foot of genius. Cherish him, Mrs. Chesterton, cherish him."

There are two photographs of him from his St. Paul's days, both of them showing him as one of a group of ten boys who, belonged to a discussion group they had founded called the Junior Debating Club, or JDC, which met every week in one of their houses, where after high tea one of them would read a paper which they then debated. They all took it with utmost seriousness, and none of them more so than Chesterton, who saw it as a paradigm of ideal friendship not unlike the Knights of the Round Table. In both photographs, Chesterton appears as a tall, robustly handsome young man who is just as formally dressed as the rest of them in his dark suit, waistcoat, stiff collar, and, in his case only—all the others are wearing four-in-hands—a bow tie. In one of the photographs the boys have arranged themselves in the form of a pyramid, at the apex of which is one who became Chesterton's great lifelong friend—E. C. Bentley by name, who one day during a boring chemistry class wrote on the blank sheet of blotting paper before him a four-line verse in what Chesterton called "that severe and stately form of Free Verse which has since become known by his own second name as 'the Clerihew.'"

Sir Humphrey Davy
Detested gravy.
He incurred the opprobrium
Of discovering sodium.

Bentley was two years younger than Chesterton, but so unusually intelligent for his age that according to Maisie Ward, "Chesterton not only admired him—as he was to do all his life—but wanted to be like him, to say the kind of thing he thought Bentley would say," and when Chesterton died in 1936, Bentley wrote his widow that theirs was "a friendship which meant more to me in my youth than I can say." On leaving St. Paul's all of Chesterton's friends including Bentley went on to Oxford or Cambridge, but Chesterton himself chose to study art at the Slade School in north London, and the three years he spent there—1892–1895—were the darkest and most terrifying of his life.

Many forces were involved. In choosing an art school instead of a university he separated himself from the JDC friends he had cherished for years, and although he and Bentley maintained a voluminous correspondence, it was a poor substitute for being together. At the same time he was no longer in close daily contact with the indulgent mother, the proud and endlessly entertaining father, and the younger brother, who was another of his great friends despite the fact, or because of it, that all their lives they argued incessantly about almost anything. As if all this was not disorienting enough, at the age of eighteen and a half he had only just emerged from puberty, with all kinds of sexual confusions and fantasies that menaced him from within no less than the cavern-dwelling goblins of George MacDonald. "A meaningless fit of depression, taking the form of certain absurd psychological worries, came upon me, and instead of dismissing it and talking to people I had it out and went very far into the abyss indeed" was the way he sanitized it in a letter to Bentley, but some forty years later in his autobiography he was able to be more forthright: "I could at the time imagine the worst and wildest disproportions and distortions of more normal passion. . . . I had an overpowering impulse to record and draw horrible ideas and images; plunging deeper and deeper as in a blind spiritual suicide." Nothing he wrote, however, evokes the horribleness of it as vividly as those images themselves as he set them down in the form of drawings in a series of notebooks he began to keep while he was still at St. Paul's and continued throughout the Slade years. According to Maisie Ward, when two of his friends happened upon one of them, they turned to each other and asked, "Is Chesterton going mad?" Again and again there is sketch of an evil face, sometimes of an angel with the face of a devil. There is one called "The Temptation," which shows a single desolate figure standing in a wilderness. There are scenes of men and woman being martyred. There are instruments of torture like swords, thongs, and scourges. There is a naked man hanging by his arms from a bar. There is evidence that there were others so appalling that he destroyed them.

"There is something truly menacing in the thought of how quickly I could imagine the maddest when I had never committed the mildest crime," he wrote in the *Autobiography*, and there is no doubt that it was to crimes of sadistic sexual violence that he referred, adding later, "I have never felt the faintest temptation to the particular madness of Wilde," which raises the question as to why, if that was the case, he felt obliged to say so. But whatever the exact nature of the tormenting fantasies, they convinced him "of the objective solidity of sin" and that "he had dug quite low enough to discover the devil." With some of his friends he was also dabbling in the occult, particularly the ouija board, until he became convinced that "we were playing with fire; or even hellfire" and gave it up because it gave him headaches as well as "what I can best describe as a bad smell in the mind." Touchingly, poignantly, even as all these things were going on, he wrote out in one of the same notebooks a little verse he called "An Idyll."

> Tea is made; the red fogs shut round the house but the gas burns.
> I wish I had at this moment round the table
> A company of fine people.
> Two of them are at Oxford and one in Scotland and two at other
>   places.
> But I wish they would all walk in now, for the tea is made.

Part of his troubles was that the decadence and darkness that horrified him in himself were also all around him in those last few years of the nineteenth century. The beliefs and values that mid-Victorian England had looked upon as eternal were giving place to doubt, skepticism, a loss of inner balance, and all that Matthew Arnold could hear of the faith of his fathers was "Its melancholy, long, withdrawing roar." Schopenhauer was in vogue, with his grim philosophy that life was nothing more than an illusory, malignant affair that inveigles humankind into reproducing in order to perpetuate it. Mr. Pickwick and the good folk of Barchester had been replaced by Dorian Gray and Svengali, and Chesterton's beloved artist G. F. Watts (about whom he did a book), with his great allegorical canvases and edifying sculptures, had been succeeded by the ambiguously sensual pen-and-ink drawings of Aubrey Beardsley for *The Yellow Book* and the misty, moonlit "Nocturnes" of Whistler. Impressionism flourished, of which Chesterton wrote that "it illustrated skepticism in the form of subjectivism . . . and lends itself to the metaphysical suggestion that things only exist as we perceive them, or that things do not exist at all."

With all of this going on in the air around him, he reached the point where "I did not very clearly distinguish between dreaming and waking; not only as a mood but as a metaphysical doubt," adding then in words reminiscent of Mark Twain's *The Mysterious Stranger,* "I felt as if everything might be a dream. It was as if I had myself projected the universe from within, with all its trees and stars; and that is so near to the notion of being God that it is manifestly even nearer to going mad." He had at this period of his life no particular religious faith to fall back on—his parents had even less—and isolated as he was from his familiar world and suspecting that the blackness he found in himself was the blackness of human nature generally, madness might indeed have been the end of it. But it wasn't, and what saved him, and how that saving came about, is what he translated into the fantastical semicomic novel that is arguably the one real masterpiece he ever produced.

The Man Who Was Thursday is its title—in the autobiography Chesterton parodies it with such possible alternatives as "The Woman Who Was Half-past Eight" and "The Cow Who Was Tomorrow Evening"—and its protagonist is a poet named Gabriel Syme, who is the author himself in thin disguise. Like Chesterton, he wears a great cloak about his shoulders and carries a sword-stick, and his name itself points in the same direction, with Gabriel close to being an anagram for Gilbert and, as is made explicit in the novel, Syme as a cockneyfied version of *same*. Gabriel Syme is the protagonist, and the enemy he contends with is virtually everybody else, including, as he comes to believe, God. The story takes the form of a dream Syme has while walking with another, redheaded poet named Gregory and his sister Rosamond through a red-brick, Bohemian suburb of London called Saffron Park, which closely resembles the Bedford Park where Chesterton's future wife Frances was living when he first met her, and the subtitle of the novel is "A Nightmare," which Chesterton complained nobody seemed to notice although it was "perhaps the only true and reliable statement in the book" and which he explains as the "nightmare of things not as they are, but as they seemed to the young half-pessimist of the nineties."

As they walk along, Syme discovers that his red-headed companion—who looks "like a walking blasphemy, a blend of the angel and the ape"—is not only a poet but also an anarchist, and when Syme asks him if that means that he wants to abolish government, his answer is, "To abolish God! . . . We wish to deny all those arbitrary distinctions between vice and virtue, honor and treachery, upon which mere rebels base themselves. . . . We have abolished Right and Wrong." What is still more, Syme discovers that Gregory is about to be elected to fill a vacancy on the Central Anarchist Council, a group of seven men named after the days of the week with their leader known as Sunday, whom Gregory describes by saying that he is by so far the greatest man in Europe that "Caesar and Napoleon would have been children in his hands." After making Syme swear by "whatever beastly thing you believe in" that he will never tell what he has seen, Gregory says that he will take him to the secret branch meeting he is on his way to at that very moment, where he will be elected the new Thursday. Only after Syme has so sworn does he confess that, just as Gregory is not only a poet but an anarchist, he, Syme, is not only a poet but a policeman, and Gregory is so horrified by the revelation that Syme comforts him by pointing out that they have now checkmated each other since after his solemn vow he is honorbound not to tell the police that Gregory is an anarchist just as Gregory cannot tell the anarchists that Syme is a policeman because then there would be hell to pay from the Central Council. They thereupon proceed to the secret meeting together, where by some very fast talking Syme manages to convince them that he is an even more ruthless anarchist than his friend, and the result is that when he is finished, it is he, not Gregory, who is elected to fill Thursday's vacancy by a landslide vote. It is just the kind of topsy-turvy, paradoxical situation that it delighted Chesterton to use in virtually all his fiction, and it is also, of course, the stuff of dreams, particularly of nightmares, where everything is always unforesee-able, ever-changing, and a little mad and where there is nothing anywhere solid and real enough to get your bearings by because everything refuses to stay put for long and nothing is ever what it seems. It is also, needless to say, very much like Chesterton's state of mind those years when he was studying at the Slade art school.

With all this established, the stage is set for the story to begin, but first Chesterton interjects a flashback chapter in which we dis-cover what kind of policeman Syme is and how he got to be one in the first place. "Being surrounded by every kind of revolt from infancy," he writes—and one thinks of the young Chesterton sur-rounded by a world where all the values and verities of an earlier period were being challenged by the decadents, the Impressionists, the Schopenhauerian nihilists, and the like, not to mention also by the darkness within himself—"Gabriel had to revolt into something so he revolted into the only thing left—sanity." He became, in other words, not an ordinary policeman, but a kind of policeman-philosopher who does not go "to pot-houses to arrest thieves . . . but to artistic parties to arrest pessimists," and the enemy, as he understands it, are not murderers who "respect human life [and] merely wish to attain a greater fullness of human life in themselves," but rather those who "hate life itself, their own as much as other people's." When Syme decides that he wants to join forces with the ones who do battle with them, he is taken to

Scotland Yard to meet the chief of police himself and is led into a room "the abrupt blackness of which startled him like a blaze of light." The brief conversation that takes place between them there is so magical that it must be quoted in full:

"Are you the new recruit?" asked a heavy voice.

And in some strange way, though there was not the shadow of a shape in the gloom, Syme knew two things: first, that it came from a man of massive stature; and second, that the man had his back to him.

"Are you the new recruit?" said the invisible chief, who seemed to have heard all about it. "All right. You are engaged."

Syme, quite swept of his feet, made a feeble fight against this irrevocable phrase.

"I really have no experience," he began.

"No one has any experience," said the other, "of the Battle of Armageddon."

"But I am really unfit—"

"You are willing, that is enough," said the unknown.

"Well, really," said Syme, "I don't know any profession of which mere willingness is the final test."

"I do," said the other—"martyrs. I am condemning you to death. Good day."

Thus ends the interview, and on his way out Syme is given a small blue card identifying him as a member of the police.

As Chesterton proceeds then to set his plot in motion with an opening tableau, one thinks of that earliest childhood memory he had of looking through the proscenium of his father's toy theater at a man on a bridge with a golden key in his hand. Although he no longer had any idea what it was all about, as he wrote years later, it continued to have for him "a sort of aboriginal authenticity impossible to describe" that haunted him for the rest of his life, and when the curtain goes up for the first time on the Central Anarchist Council assembled together in one place, the sight of them produces much the same effect. They are having an early breakfast meeting not in secret behind locked doors, but in broad daylight on a hotel balcony overlooking Leicester Square because of Sunday's "notion of concealing ourselves by not concealing ourselves" (later to be made much of by Father Brown in his sleuthing) and its corollary "that if you didn't seem to be hiding nobody hunted you out." No less than the man with the golden key, they are like figures in a dream as they sit there around the table, but it is a dream so vivid that for as long as it lasts there is no questioning their own aboriginal authenticity. They could not be more different from one another, and yet they have one thing in common, which is that each has something about him that Syme finds terrifying. In the case of Sunday, it is his sheer size.

Syme's first thought was that the weight of him must break down the balcony of stone. His vastness did not lie only in the fact that he was abnormally tall and quite incredibly fat. This man was planned enormously in his original proportions, like a statue carved deliberately as colossal. His head, crowned with white hair, as seen from behind looked bigger than a head ought to be. The ears that stood out from it looked larger than human ears. He was enlarged terribly to scale; and this sense of size was so staggering, that when Syme saw him all the other figures seemed quite suddenly to dwindle and become dwarfish. They were still sitting there as before with their flowers and frock coats, but now it looked as if the big man was entertaining five children to tea.

His face was equally colossal, and as Syme approached, it seemed to grow larger and larger so that he "was gripped with a fear that when he was quite close [it] would be too big to be possible, and that he would scream aloud."

And then the other five: Monday, the council's secretary, has a long, pale, intellectual face—"ascetic yet in its way noble"—but at the same time his spasm of a lopsided smile is nightmarish. Tuesday is a man named Gogol with a thick Polish accent who seems more or less normal with his "bewildering bush of brown hair and beard," except that his terrier-like eyes peering out of the tangle give him the grotesque look of a dog or cat in a satin tie and high white collar. Wednesday is the Marquis de St. Eustache, "the only man at the table who wore his fashionable clothes as if they were his own," but his mouth through his blue-black beard is sensual and scornful and his crimson lips cruel. Professor de Worms, Friday, has the air of a man who "save for his intellect . . . is in the last dissolution of senile decay" and is so decrepit that it makes Syme fear "that whenever [he] moved, a leg or arm might fall off." And finally Saturday, "the simplest and the most baffling of all." He is a doctor by the name of Bull with a square, dark, clean-shaven face, about whom there was nothing odd whatever except that he wore a pair of dark, almost opaque spectacles that made Syme suspect "that his eyes might be covered up because they were too frightful to see" and that he was just possibly "the wickedest of all those wicked men." The reason for their meeting, Syme discovers, is to plot the assassination of the czar, who is due to be in Paris in three days' time—the black-bearded Marquis is to do it with a bomb—and as Syme fixes his gaze upon the huge figure of Sunday "with his large plans, which were too obvious to be detected, with his large face, which was too frank to be understood," the main action begins.

The dedication of the novel to Edmund Clerihew Bentley is accompanied by a long poem to him containing the following lines:

A cloud was on the minds of men, and wailing went the weather.
Yea, a sick cloud upon the soul when we were boys together.
Science announced nonentity and art admired decay;
The world was old and ended, but you and I were gay.
. . . .

Children we were—our forts of sand were even as weak as we,
High as they went we piled them up to break that bitter sea.
Fools as we were in motley, all jangling and absurd,
When all church bells were silent our cap and bells were heard.
. . . .

This is a tale of those old fears, even of those emptied hells,
And none but you shall understand the true thing that it tells—
Of what colossal gods of shame could cow men and yet crash,
Of what huge devils hid the stars, yet fell at a pistol flash.

The element of surprise is so much a part of the novel's antic power that it is impossible to describe what *happens* in it without the risk of ruining it for those who have never read it, but because there are those who may never read it at all unless enticed by some sense of the unique outlandishness of what awaits them, it seems important—without quite giving away the whole show—to say at least that it is a comedy in the sense of the poem's motley, cap, and bells, and yet also in Dante's sense, because what mainly happens is a series of chapters in which one by one the huge devils fall and finally what is taken to be the colossal god of shame himself goes crashing.

The process begins there on the balcony in Leicester Square, where over their bacon and eggs the six men sworn to destroy the world are discussing the fate of the czar. As the meeting progresses, Syme becomes increasingly aware that Sunday, who has been mostly silent, is staring forward with great intensity and that what he is staring at is Syme himself, who of course is terrified that his imposture has somehow been discovered. When down below among the sunlit trees on the square he notices the motionless figure of a policeman—"a pillar of common sense and order"—his impulse is to leap over the stone balustrade and race to him for help, but what restrains him is the vow he made to the poet Gregory and the sense that his "antiquated honor" obliges him to conceal his true identity to the end even if it means falling into the hands of "the great enemy of mankind, whose very intellect was a torture chamber." And then the dreaded moment occurs. Sunday halts the discussion about the czar by bidding them all to follow him into a private room, and Syme is sure that his doom is about to be sealed. All further planning of the assassination is to be postponed to some other occasion, Sunday says, because he has discovered that one of their number is a traitor, and Syme has already started to rise out of his chair with his finger on the trigger of his loaded revolver when Sunday flaps "his large flat hand like the fin of some huge fish" and announces that the name of the traitor is Gogol—"that hairy humbug over there who pretends to be a Pole." At Sunday's command the man who until now has been Tuesday produces a little blue card identical to the one Syme was given at Scotland Yard and at the same time rips off his false whiskers and shaggy wig beneath which is a pale man with thin red hair and no Polish accent at all but a faintly cockney one. What makes the scene so successful is that, like a good joke, its climax comes upon the reader as unexpectedly as upon Syme. Beyond that, again like a good joke, not only is its power to enchant undiminished even after many hearings have robbed it of all surprise, but as it is told and retold in different forms throughout the ensuing pages, the comedy and fun of it come closer and closer to divine comedy in the sense of leading us to the final chapters whose revelation is not a joke at all, but a kind of flaming apocalypse in which unmasking itself is unmasked.

We are as deceived by Gogol's hairy disguise as Syme is, mistaking what is entirely an illusion for what is entirely real, and that is part of the joke. The other part is that we are equally given to taking reality itself as merely illusory, and Chesterton is at his motley best in making that point in the case of the tottering wreck that is Professor de Worms. Although the weather at Leicester Square was warm and sunny enough to make possible an alfresco breakfast, in the manner of dreams it suddenly seems to be winter, and Syme finds that it is beginning to snow as he comes upon the Professor with the white drift rising around his ankles as he stands gazing at the wax head of a lady in a hairdresser's shop window. Thankful that the old man's elaborate limp and snail's pace of a walk will make it impossible for him to follow, Syme finds his way to a small restaurant in Soho and after lunching there moves to a wine shop below, where to his astonishment he finds the Professor hunched over a glass of milk. Chesterton knew and loved his native London well and describes in such detail that it could be plotted on a city map how Syme's continued flight through the snow storm, which by now has become blinding, takes him in the direction of Covent Garden to a tea shop in Fleet Street—he has just ordered coffee when the Professor comes hobbling in through the door—and then, by a mad hundred-yard dash, onto the open upper deck of a passing omnibus, where he hears the labored, asthmatic breathing of his nemesis as he struggles up the steep stair to wrap himself in a waterproof rug. On then as fast as his legs will carry him to Ludgate Circus, up Ludgate Hill, around St. Paul's cathedral, and along Cheapside toward the river, where he takes refuge in a sinister dockside pub only seconds before the Professor comes staggering in yet again, sits down across the table from him, orders yet another glass of milk, and then asks him if he is a policeman. Syme denies it passionately again and again despite the old man's shrill persistence, until finally, "with insane calm," he says one last time, "I am not in the British police," and the Professor replies, "That's a pity," falling back in his chair, "because I am," thereupon reaching into his waistcoat pocket and taking out a blue card exactly like Gogol's and Syme's. All Syme can do is throw back his head in a burst of laughter at the thought that "this devil from whom he had been fleeing all along was only an elder brother of his own house . . . only the shadow of a friend trying to catch him up," and for a moment the whole mad world comes right again. When they compare notes later, the impostor tells about the officer who originally commissioned him as a policeman, but says he cannot describe him.

Syme interrupts him. "I know," he said, "because you talked to him in a dark room."

Once again the joke has to do with mistaking the friend for the enemy, the sham for the real, but then comes the joke within the joke when the man beneath the disguise—a professional actor named Wilks—describes in one of the novel's richest comic passages what happened when he and the real de Worms, a German nihilist professor, came face to face and the joke is told in reverse. As a lark, and because he disliked the old man, Wilks decided to try impersonating him and so utterly succeeded with a room full of his supporters that when the real de Worms came in, the following scene took place:

The pessimists all around me looked anxiously from one Professor to the other Professor to see which was really the more feeble. But I won. An old man in poor health, like my rival, could not be expected to be so impressively feeble as a young actor in the prime of life. You see, he really had paralysis, and working within this definite limitation, he couldn't be so jolly paralytic as I was. Then he tried to blast my claims intellectually. I countered that by a very simple dodge. Whenever he said something that nobody but he could understand, I replied with something which I could not even understand myself. "I don't fancy," he said, "that you could have worked out the principle that evolution is only negation, since there inheres in it the introduction of lacunae, which are an essential of differentiation." I replied quite scornfully, "You read all that up in Pinckwerts; the notion that involution functioned eugenically was exposed long ago by Glumpe." It is unnecessary for me to say that there never were such people as Pinckwerts and Glumpe. But the people all around (rather to my surprise) seemed to remember them quite well, and the Professor, finding that the learned and mysterious method left him rather at the mercy of an enemy slightly deficient in scruples, fell back upon a more popular form of wit. "I see," he sneered, "you prevail like the false pig in Aesop." "And you fail," I answered, smiling, "like the hedgehog in Montaigne." Need I say that there is no hedgehog in Montaigne? "Your claptrap comes off," he said; "so would your beard." I had no intelligent answer to this, which was quite true and rather witty. But I laughed heartily, answered, "Like the Pantheist's boots," at random, and turned on my heel with all the honours of victory. The real Professor was thrown out, but not with violence, though one man tried very patiently to pull off his nose. He is now, I believe, received everywhere in Europe as a delightful impostor. His apparent earnestness and anger, you see, make him all the more entertaining.

All of this is Chesterton having enormous fun, but even in the midst of it he is doing more than that. By the time Syme in his flight from the bogus Professor has entered Ludgate Circus, the sunset has turned a sickly green and bronze, but even so there is still light enough for him to see St. Paul's, and the description of it is a reminder that drawing and painting were Chesterton's first love. "Right up against these dreary colors rose the black bulk of the cathedral; and upon the top of the cathedral was a random splash and great stain of snow, still clinging as to an Alpine peak. It had fallen accidentally, but just so fallen as to half drape the dome from its very topmost point, and to pick out in perfect silver the great orb and the cross. When Syme saw it he suddenly straightened, and made with his sword-stick an involuntary salute."

With the Professor as an embodiment of evil on his heels, he realizes that "the devils might have captured heaven, but they had not yet captured the cross," and for the moment at least he is filled with the same courage that he felt during the original meeting of the council in Leicester Square. Syme had just heard the Professor make the grim pronouncement that "Every man knows in his heart that nothing is worth doing" and was convinced that he himself was about to be destroyed by Sunday as a fraud when he heard the strains of a hurdy-gurdy from the street below "full of the vivacity, the vulgarity, and the irrational valor of the poor." It gave him new heart by reassuring him both that he was somehow "the ambassador of all those common and kindly people in the street, who every day marched into battle to the music of the barrel-organ" and also that it was the barrel organ and not Sunday that was somehow, in spite of everything, ultimately right. Syme's valor was nonetheless quite as irrational as the poor's in the sense that everything he saw as he sat there among the anarchists seemed living proof that the world was as lost as Chesterton himself believed it to be during the Slade years, and Syme's problem, no less than it had been Chesterton's, is where to find hope. Indeed, in a world threatened by Sunday can there be any hope at all? The answer, of course, depends on who Sunday is, and that is what the final chapters of the novel explore.

The difficulty in writing about *The Man Who Was Thursday* is that the scenes are so richly rendered that the temptation is simply to let them speak for themselves by quoting them, and none of them more so than the ones leading up to Sunday's unmasking. The six members of the Central Anarchist Council, who through a series of nightmare-like adventures have by now discovered that they are all of them blue card–carrying policemen, decide to confront him once and for all at their next general meeting. "We are six men going to ask one man what he means," Dr. Bull says—the man who had been Saturday—to which Syme replies, "I think it is six men going to ask one man what they mean."

In any case they find that Sunday is already waiting for them on the balcony when they reach Leicester Square. He is reading a newspaper as they make their way across the street, and yet they approach "as if they were watched out of heaven by a hundred eyes." Unpredictable as always, he welcomes them not with some unnerving display of power but, even more unnervingly, with a smile as radiant as the morning sun. "Delightful!" is the word he greets them with, and when they tell him that they have not assassinated the czar, he seems scarcely to hear them, but banters on for a while, making foolish little jokes, until finally Syme is the one to come out with it and ask him directly what he is.

"I? What am I?" roared the President, and he rose slowly to an incredible height, like some enormous wave about to crash above them and break. "You want to know what I am, do you? . . . You will understand the sea, and I shall still be a riddle; you shall know what the stars are, and not know what I am. Since the beginning of the world all men have hunted me like a wolf—kings and sages, and poets and law-givers, all the churches, and all the philosophers. But I have never been caught yet, and the skies will fall in the time I turn to bay. I have given them a good run for their money, and I will now."

And then, just as he has swung "like some huge orang-outang" over the balustrade of the balcony, he thrusts his chin over the edge and solemnly says that he will tell them one thing. The thing he tells them is that he and the man in the dark who made than all policemen are one and the same.

The first time I read the book I was fourteen years old and sick in bed with a cold in the Lawrenceville School infirmary—my eye had been caught by the crazy title—and although I have read it at least a dozen times since over the years, the revelation still comes upon me as no less fathomlessly suggestive than it seemed to me then and still shimmering with surprise. The one who seemed the world's worst enemy turns out to be the world's staunchest defender. The voice in the impenetrable dark is also the voice of the monster reading his newspaper in the dazzling sunlight. The one they had all been battling against in the name of human decency and sanity unmasks himself as the one who had signed them up to do battle in the first place, and thus the joke of all the earlier unmaskings is transcended by a joke so vast and simple that none of them had understood it. Nor does Sunday make it any more understandable as he leads them then on a never to be forgotten chase through London. First in a cab, then in a fire engine, then on the back of an elephant from the Zoological Gardens, then in a hot-air balloon from the Earl's Court Exhibition, he bounds along "like a great ball of india-rubber" with the six of them in hot pursuit while from time to time he scatters little slips of paper with sublime messages on them like "Fly at once. The truth about your trouser-stretchers is known—A FRIEND," and "Your beauty has not left me indifferent—From LITTLE SNOWDROP."

In the course of the chase, Syme's light gray suit is ruined—"His silk hat was broken over his nose by a swinging bough, his coat-tails were torn to the shoulder by arresting thorns, the clay of England was splashed up to his collar"—and, unlike one another as they are in virtually every way, it is hard not to think of him in conjunction with the "listless stranger" in Hopkins' "Epithalamion" taking off his clothes to swim in the woodland pond and Huck and Jim bare as birth on their raft. In each case it seems to be that in order for new things to start happening, old things have to be laid aside. In his nakedness the stranger finds that he is listless no more, but "looks about him, laughs, swims" in the transfiguring, "kindcold" water, and Huck and Jim, having stripped themselves no less of their respective forms of bondage than of their cloth-ing, float down the mighty waters of the Mississippi to discover new freedom. Similarly, when Gabriel Syme and his five companions come at last to the "long, low house, mellow in the mild light of sunset," which is where Sunday lives—mysteriously it reminds them all of their boyhoods and summons up memories earlier than the memory of their own mothers—they put their former clothes aside, and a servant gives all of them costumes to wear to the great fancy dress ball that he tells them is to take place that night. The one Syme is given is blue and gold embroidered with the sun and the moon, because according to Genesis it was on Thursday, the fourth day, that the sun and moon were first created, and thus, freshly attired, he sets forth into the mystery that has brought them all here.

The ball takes place in an old English garden, and as Syme looks about at the great crowd of guests dancing by the flickering light of torches and bonfires, he sees that they are costumed to represent virtually every shape in nature, a scene consciously reminiscent of the concluding chapters of the book of Job, which Chesterton had written an introduction to just the year before:

There was a man dressed as a windmill with enormous sails, a man dressed as an elephant, a man dressed as a balloon; the two last, together, seemed to keep the thread of their farcical adventures. Syme even saw, with a queer thrill, one dancer dressed like an enormous hornbill, with a beak twice as big as himself—the queer bird which had fixed itself on his fancy like a living question while he was rushing down the long road at the Zoological Gardens. There were a thousand other such objects, however. There was dancing lamp-post, a dancing apple tree, a dancing ship. One would have thought that the untamable tune of some mad musician had set all the common objects of field and street dancing an eternal jig.

On a green bank at one end of the garden there are seven great chairs, the thrones of the seven days, and one by one, to the wild cheering of the dancers, Syme and his companions take their places in them until only the central one is empty. Just as someone has expressed the fear that maybe Sunday was killed when the balloon came down, Syme sees on the faces in front of him "a frightful and beautiful change" reflecting the appearance behind him of Sunday, who silently takes his seat, "draped plainly, in a pure and terrible white, and his hair . . . like a silver flame on his forehead." The ball continues at full force for what seem hours until little by little the masqueraders disappear into the house, the fires fade, the stars come out, and finally the seven are left alone on their thrones, none of them having as yet spoken a word. It is Sunday who breaks the silence, "but so dreamily that he might have been continuing a conversation rather than beginning one," and in this speech Chesterton comes closer than anywhere else in the novel to describing how he managed to survive at the time when—in the words of the dedicatory poem to Bentley—"a sick cloud" had been upon his soul and "those old fears . . . those emptied hells" had nearly been the end of him.

"We will eat and drink later," he said. "Let us remain together a little, we who have loved each other so sadly, and have fought so long. I seem to remember only centuries of heroic war, in which you were always the heroes—epic on epic, iliad on iliad, and you always brothers in arms. Whether it was but recently (for time is nothing), or at the beginning of the world, I sent you out to war. I sat in the darkness, where there is not any created thing, and to you I was only a voice commanding valour and an unnatural virtue. You heard the voice in the dark, and you never heard it again. The sun in heaven denied it, the earth and sky denied it, all human wisdom denied it. And when I met you in the daylight I denied it myself. . . . But you were men. You did not forget your secret honour, though the whole cosmos turned an engine of torture to tear it out of you. . . ."

There was complete silence in the starlit garden, and then the black-browed Secretary, implacable, turned in his chair towards Sunday, and said in a harsh voice—

"Who and what are you?"

"I am the Sabbath," said the other one without moving. "I am the peace of God."

In his autobiography Chesterton wrote that Sunday was intended to represent not so much God as "Nature as it appears to the pantheist, whose pantheism is struggling out of pessimism," but it is evident that he was not altogether sure about this. "You tear off the mask of Nature and you find God," he said elsewhere, and then there is a penultimate scene under the stars where Chesterton seems to discover almost in spite of himself that at a level beneath conscious purpose he had contrived the mystery of Sunday to be deeper than he knew.

Dressed all in black with a sword at his side, the ape-faced Lucian Gregory suddenly appears, the Saffron Park poet who had originally precipitated Syme's entire nightmare and who, as things turn out, is the one and only true anarchist. Full of hate and with his red hair flaming, he curses Sunday, more than for anything else, for never having known the agony that he, Gregory, had suffered, and it is Syme who, remembering the agony of his own nightmare, confronts Sunday with the charge directly.

"Have you," he cried in a dreadful voice, "have you ever suffered?"

As he gazed, the great face grew to an awful size, grew larger than the colossal mask of Memnon, which had made him scream as a child. It grew larger and larger, filling the whole sky; then everything went black. Only in the blackness before it entirely destroyed his brain he seemed to hear a distant voice saying a commonplace text that he had heard somewhere, "Can ye drink of the cup that I drink of?"

Apparently Chesterton worried that people would accuse him of making everything end on too positive a note with Sunday in his heaven and all right with the world. He did not want his fantasy to suggest that sin and evil have no real existence, that they are merely illusions as deceptive as Gogol's false whiskers or the terrifying black spectacles of Dr. Bull. Lucian Gregory is there to indicate that, on the contrary, evil persists and is as real as Sunday is, but the matter was still troubling him when he wrote some twenty years later, "I should not want it supposed, as some I think have supposed, that in resisting the heresy of pessimism I implied the equally morbid and diseased insanity of optimism. I was not [in the novel] considering whether anything is really evil, but whether everything is really evil." He did not wish it supposed that we perceive evil as a reality simply because, as Syme says, "We have only known the back of the world . . . and it looks brutal," whereas from the front its face is like—Sunday's. "His face frightened me, as it did everyone," Syme says, "but not because it was evil. On the contrary, it frightened me because it was so beautiful, so good."

The writing of a book can be like the dreaming of a dream—especially a book whose subtitle is *A Nightmare*—and when that is the case, books, like dreams, can be thought of as bearing a message to the reader from the writer's subconscious or whatever it is in the writer that the dream comes from. But also, like dreams, books can on occasion bear a message from a remoter and more mysterious region still, and in that case they become a message not just *from* the writer but also *to* the writer, revealing things that the writer was not fully aware of knowing before. It seems to me that these concluding scenes at the fancy dress ball are a case in point and that in the process of writing them Chesterton discovered a previously unsuspected depth of beauty and goodness in the figure of Sunday which—along with the influence of his new young wife, Frances—had much to do with his moving from a vague religiosity to becoming a true believer and ultimately a devoted member and champion of the Catholic Church. He wrote years later how a distinguished psychiatrist once said to him, "I know a number of men who nearly went mad but were saved because they really understood *The Man Who Was Thursday*," and the reason he so treasured the remark was his realization that one of the madmen who had been saved was himself.

It was undoubtedly the first stirrings of this renewed and deepened faith that helped him survive his near breakdown, but there was also the influence upon him of two writers whom he alludes to in the dedicatory poem to Bentley, the first of them in these lines:

> *Not all unhelped we held the fort, our tiny flags unfurled;*
> *Some giants laboured in that cloud to lift it from the world.*
> *I find again the book we found, I feel the hour that flings*
> *Far out of fish-shaped Paumanok some cry of cleaner things;*
> *And the Green Carnation withered, as in forest fires that pass,*
> *Roared in the wind of all the world ten million leaves of grass.*

Paumanok, the Indian name for Long Island, where he was born, and "leaves of grass" refer, of course, to Walt Whitman—he died toward the end of Chesterton's time at the Slade school—whose work he had been introduced to by one of his JDC friends while still at St. Paul's and who did so much to save his sanity that "with the understanding that is love and the love that is laughter" he wrote a parody of him, as good as any poem he ever did, in the form of a variation on "Old King Cole":

> *Me clairvoyant,*
> *Me conscious of you, old camarado,*
> *Needing no telescope, lorgnette, field-glass,*
> *opera-glass, myopic pince-nez,*
> *Me piercing two thousand years with eye naked and not ashamed;*

The crown cannot hide you from me;
Musty old feudal-heraldic trappings cannot hide you from me,
I perceive that you drink.
(I am drinking with you. I am as drunk as you are).
I see you are inhaling tobacco, puffing, smoking, spitting
(I do not object to your spitting).
You prophetic of American largeness,
You anticipating the broad masculine manners of these States,
I see in you also there are movements, tremors, tears,
desire for the melodious;
I salute your three violinists, endlessly making vibrations,
Rigid, relentless, capable of going on for ever;
They play my accompaniment; but I shall take no notice of any
*   accompaniment;*
I myself am a complete orchestra.
So long.

But behind the laughter there was enormous appreciation of the man whose roaring affirmation of life and the world and humankind in all its endless variety provided such a welcome antidote to the negativism and ennui of the 1890s.

The other writer was Robert Louis Stevenson, who appears in the lines "Or sane and sweet and sudden as a bird sings in the rain— / Truth out of Tusitala spoke and pleasure out of pain. / Yes, cool and clear and sudden as a bird sings in the grey, / Dunedin to Samoa spoke, and darkness unto day," where Tusitala is a reference to the name Stevenson was given when he lived in Samoa, and Dunedin to his birthplace, Edinburgh. In the section of Chesterton's biography of him that deals with his student days among the pessimists and nihilists of Paris, he writes that "He stood up among all these things and shook himself with a sort of impatient sanity; a shrug of scepticism about scepticism. His real distinction is that he had the sense to see that there is nothing to be done with Nothing," and there seems no reason to doubt that it was from this aspect of Stevenson that he particularly took heart and that in describing him here, he was describing himself.

By the summer of 1894, the year he turned twenty, Chesterton had more or less recovered from his own personal nightmare, left art school, and decided that he might possibly turn instead to a career in writing. According to Maisie Ward, from that time on he liked to call himself "always perfectly happy," and the notebook he kept at the time suggests that it was not entirely an exaggeration. Having been given back his life and sanity, he was filled with both an enormous sense of thankfulness and an enormous need for someone or something to thank, which he expressed in a number of the random pieces that the notebook contains, including the following three:

> You say grace before meals.
> All right.
> But I say grace before the play and the opera,
> And grace before the concert and the pantomime,
> And grace before I open a book,
> And grace before sketching, painting,
> Swimming fencing, boxing, walking, playing, dancing;
> And grace before I dip the pen in the ink.

THE PRAYER OF A MAN WALKING
I thank thee, O Lord, for the stones in the street.
I thank thee for the hay-carts yonder and for the houses built and
  half-built
That fly past me as I stride.
But most of all for the great wind in my nostrils
As if thine own nostrils were close.

THE PRAYER OF A MAN RESTING
The twilight closes round me,
My head is bowed before the Universe.
I thank thee, O Lord, for a child I knew seven years ago
And whom I have never seen since.

It was at this time also that he met Frances Blogg, whom, after a long engagement, he married in 1901. During the engagement, Frances' sister Gertrude was killed in a bicycle accident, and she was so prostrated with grief that directly after the funeral she went to Italy to recover. At the funeral, all the flowers were white except for the ones that Chesterton sent, which were brilliant scarlet and orange and accompanied by a card that read, "He that maketh His angels spirits and His ministers a flame of fire." While Frances was in Italy, he also wrote her a remarkable letter that further reveals the near euphoria that followed in the wake of the Slade years' nightmare. "I do not think there is anyone who takes quite such a fierce pleasure in things being themselves as I do. The startling wetness of water excites and intoxicates me; the fieriness of fire, the steeliness of steel, the unutterable muddiness of mud. . . . I will not ask you to forgive this rambling levity. I, for one, have sworn, by the sword of God that has struck us, and before the beautiful face of the dead, that the first joke that occurred to me I would make, the first nonsense poem I thought of I would write, that I would begin again *at once* with a heavy heart at times, as to other duties, to the duty of being perfectly silly, perfectly trivial, and as far as possible, amusing. I have sworn that Gertrude should *not* feel, wherever she is, that the comedy has gone out of our theatre." And in another letter to her, "All good things are one thing. Sunsets, schools of philosophy, cathedrals, operas, mountains, horses, poems—all these are mainly disguises. One thing is always walking among us in fancy-dress, in the grey cloak of a church or the green cloak of a meadow." Finally, this same year of 1899, he described himself to Frances in the third person as one who writes in his diary, "All his passion and longing, all his queer religion, his dark and dreadful gratitude to God . . . the joy that comes on him sometimes (he cannot help it!) at the sacred intoxication of existence . . . the unconquered adoration of goodness, that dark virtue that every man has, and hides deeper than all his vices!"

It is interesting to consider what it may have been that in the midst of this almost mystical state of exaltation led him around 1907 to relive in *The Man Who Was Thursday* what he described as the "maddening horror of unreality" that had so nearly devastated him some fourteen years earlier. There was apparently a history of depression in the Blogg family—it was a constant source of worry to Chesterton that Frances herself to some extent suffered from it—and Frances' only brother, Knollys, had for years been given to periods of what she called "black despair." She and Chesterton together with her one surviving sister, Ethel, did all they could to help him, he was eventually received into the Catholic Church, and when he recovered from an unusually severe depressive episode they felt they had reason to hope that he was out of it once and for all. Then one August evening in 1906 he drowned himself off Seaford on the Sussex coast, and possibly the horror of that was what prompted his brother-in-law—for Frances' sake as well as for his own—to write his masterpiece, first published in 1908, with its phantasmagorical account of how he had encountered horror once before and managed to stare it down.

Walking through the green fields of Surrey to the house where the fancy-dress ball later takes place, Syme talks to himself about Sunday. "When I see the horrible back, I am sure that the noble face is a mask," he says. "When I see the face but for an instant, I know the back is only a jest." He then adds, "Bad is so bad, that we cannot but think good an accident; good is so good, that we feel certain that evil could be explained," and Chesterton himself, although he ate too much, drank too much, smoked too much, talked too much, nonetheless found time to devote prodigious amounts of time and passion to the explaining. In the words of the *Song of Roland*, which Syme quotes, he spent the rest of his life proclaiming that *"Païens ont tort et Chrétiens ont droit"* and, further still, that not only are pagans wrong and Christians right, but that Christianity is the last, best hope for humankind.

PART 4

WILLIAM SHAKESPEARE: THE WEIGHER OF SADNESS

William Shakespeare was christened in the Stratford church on April 26, 1564, and because as a rule christenings followed birth by several days and also because there could be no more auspicious day for England's great national poet to come into the world than the feast day of England's great patron saint, it is generally said that he was born on April 23. England was afflicted at the time by the worst plague since the Black Death, so that by September of that year one out of every fifteen people in the parish was infected, but the Shakespeares, including the new baby, were spared.

His mother was born Mary Arden, the daughter of a rich farmer from nearby Wilmcote, and his father was John Shakespeare, by trade a glover and whitawer, or dresser of soft, white leather, who kept the borough accounts for three or four years and was prosperous enough to have loaned the town money on several occasions. A year after his son's birth he was chosen one of the Stratford aldermen and a few years after that became High Bailiff and thus one of the town's most important citizens. Less than ten years later, however, when William was entering adolescence, he fell on evil times—he was behind in his taxes, owed money, stopped attending meetings of the corporation—and in 1586 was removed from the board of aldermen altogether.

As to William's education, no records survive, but the assumption is that he was sent to the King's New School on Church Street, the only grammar school for miles around, and there, according to his friend and rival playwright Ben Jonson, he learned his "small Latine and lesse Greek." At the age of eighteen he married Anne Hathaway, who was a member of a locally prominent family from nearby Shottery and whose father, a farmer, had twice been bailed out of debt by John Shakespeare. She was seven or eight years older than her new young husband, and about six months after the marriage gave birth to the first of their three children, a daughter whom they named Susanna. Susanna was followed three years later by twins christened Hamnet and Judith, presumably after Hamnet and Judith Sadler, who were among the Shakespeares' near neighbors. Hamnet Sadler—the name was interchangeable in those days with Hamlet, in which form it appears in Shakespeare's will—was a baker, and in the will, which he witnessed, Shakespeare left him, together with several other old friends, twenty-six shillings and eight pence to buy a memorial ring.

There are various legends about what Shakespeare did during the first year or two of his marriage—one of them is that he poached deer on the estate of Sir Thomas Lucy of Cherlecot and had to get out of town to escape prosecution, and another that, according to the antiquarian and biographer John Aubrey, who could have known people who had known him, he was "a school-master in the countrey"—but there is no hard evidence for any of them, and all that is sure is that at the age of twenty-one or so, with a wife and three babies to support, he left for London to seek his fortune and by 1592, when he turned twenty-eight, was beginning to be known as an actor and rising playwright. Four years later his only son, Hamnet, died at the age of eleven.

As an actor he became a member of the Lord Chamberlain's Company, later to be known as the King's Men, which, under the patronage of James I, was by far the most favored of the acting companies, and eventually he bought shares in the Globe Theater, where many of his plays were produced, with him reportedly taking minor parts in some of them like the Ghost in *Hamlet* or old Adam in *As You Like It*. His first published works were long, semi-erotic poems—*Venus and Adonis* and *The Rape of Lucrece*—both dedicated to a beautiful young man, nine years his junior, named Henry Wriothesley, the third Earl of Southampton. As to the plays, starting in 1590 they seem to have been written at the rate of about two a year. In addition to that, he must also have been almost unimaginably busy as an actor and theater manager. In good times, when the plague or other considerations hadn't closed the theaters down, a company acted every afternoon except Sundays and during Lent, presenting a different play every day of the week so that an actor had to take on a great many parts every year and was obliged to keep an unbelievable number of lines in his head. It has been estimated that leading actors like Edward Alleyn and Richard Burbage memorized about eight hundred of them for each part they played, which meant keeping some forty-eight hundred in mind every week. Aubrey says that "He was wont to go to his native Countrey once a yeare," but the repertory playing was so time-consuming that it may well have been less.

In any case, about a year after Hamnet's death, he bought one of the grandest houses in Stratford, known as New Place, and moved his wife and two daughters into it. It was not until about 1610, when he was approaching his mid-forties, that he gave up London as a place of residence and settled down to spend more or less the rest of his days in Stratford, where he invested wisely in real estate and interested himself in such local affairs as a bill for the improvement of highways in 1611 and a proposed enclosure of the open fields of Welcombe in 1614. By this time not only had his parents both died but so had three sisters and three brothers, leaving him and his younger sister Joan the sole survivors of the family. In 1607 his daughter Susanna was married to a physician named John Hall, who came from a well-to-do Bedfordshire family and had his master's degree from Cambridge. The next year they produced their one child—a daughter named Elizabeth—who was the only grandchild Shakespeare lived to see. Six years later Susanna was involved in a bizarre law case in which she sued a drunken rowdy named John Lane for having slanderously accused her of sexual misconduct with another man, but when Lane failed to show up in court, the case was dismissed.

In January of 1616 Shakespeare called in Francis Collins, a friend and attorney, in order to sketch out a draft of his will because his second daughter, Judith, had announced her intention of marrying a vintner named Thomas Quiney, and he wanted to leave her a marriage portion. On February 10 they were married, and—to add yet another family scandal—the very next month it came out that Quiney's former mistress had died in childbirth and Quiney was accused of fornication before Stratford's church court only to be let off with no more than a fine of five shillings to be given to the parish poor.

Collins came back two months later on March 25, bringing with him the completed will. Shakespeare validated the first two pages by signing them both on the bottom and then on the third and last went further still by writing, "By me William Shakespeare" instead of just his signature. Whatever he was dying of had evidently already left its mark on him because, although the words "By me William" are firm enough and clear, the "Shakespeare" wavers off into near illegibility. He died only a few weeks later on April 23, 1616—his fifty-second birthday if you accept the tradition that he was born on St. George's Day—and was buried in the chancel of Stratford's Holy Trinity Church near the north wall.

Eventually a monument was erected there, presumably commissioned by the immediate family, who must have considered the likeness acceptable. Shakespeare is depicted as standing, but with only the upper half of his body showing. He has a quill pen in his right hand, and there is a piece of paper under his left; both hands rest on a cushion. Consistent with the universally recognizable Droeshout portrait, which represents him as a comparatively young man, the sculptor shows him with a high, domed forehead, arching brows, and a moustache, but the neatly trimmed beard is more ample than the scanty under-lip one of his youth, and he has clearly put on weight, with his round, fat cheeks and thick neck, no longer the "handsome well shap't man," as someone described him to John Aubrey. No one knows whether it was Shakespeare himself or someone else who composed the rhyme carved on his grave slab—"Good frend for Jesus sake forbeare, / To digg the dust encloased here: / Bleste be the man that spares these stones, / And curst be he that moves my bones"—but in either case the injunction has been honored to this day. A fitter inscription would have been the words his friend Ben Jonson wrote of him—"Hee was (indeed) honest, of an open and free nature: had an excellent *Phantsie*; brave notions, and gentle expressions," and then "I loved the man and do honour his memory, on this side idolatry, as much as any."

Such facts as these are more or less all that is known of the life of this man who left such an extraordinary mark on the world, and yet in comparison with what is known of virtually every one of his literary contemporaries they amount to a good deal, considering that in the case of even the high-profile Ben Jonson, for instance, his date and place of birth, the name of his wife, and the number of his children have all been lost. But who Shakespeare was inside himself, as a human being, can only be guessed at from the works he left behind and particularly from *King Lear*, which more than any of them seems to have come straight from his heart.

My guess is that what makes it the most moving of the tragedies is that it is the one Shakespeare himself was most moved by as he wrote it. I would guess also that what drew him to the story of the old king and his daughters in the first place was that in Elizabethan terms he was on the threshold of old age himself and that his relationship with his own Judith and Susanna for one reason or another so preoccupied him that the complex father-daughter bond became an almost obsessive theme in his last plays. "The weight of this sad time we must obey, / Speak what we feel, not what we ought to say" are among the words, spoken by the Duke of Albany, that bring the final curtain down, and it is hard to escape the sense that in them Shakespeare is describing precisely what in writing this most feeling of all his plays he had done himself. Beneath the level of Lear's sad story, one senses, are bits and pieces of Shakespeare's own sad story, including his father's fall from glory, which he had witnessed as a boy, the death of his eleven-year-old son, and whatever wounds remained from his tangled relationship with the beautiful young man, the Dark Lady, and the Rival Poet of the sonnets. Farther beneath still, "The weight of these sad times" suggests the sadness of time itself, and it is because he was bold enough and honest enough to speak what he most deeply *felt* about that sadness that *Lear*, alone among the tragedies, has the power to bring tears to our eyes as it must surely have brought them also to his.

As to Albany's "what we ought to say," my guess is that what Shakespeare meant was that he ought to have ended it the way all the others did who had in one form or another told it before him, including Edmund Spenser in his *Faery Queene*, Camden, Geoffrey of Monmouth, the unknown author of *The Chronicle History of King Leir*, a play that preceded Shakespeare's by some ten years or so, and also his favorite historical source, Holinshed, who concluded his account with the words: "Leir and his daughter Cordeilla . . . fought with their enimies, and discomfited them in battlell . . . and then was Leir restored to his kingdome, which he ruled after this by the space of two yeeres and then died, forty yeeres after he first began to reigne." In other words, Shakespeare seems to be saying that, like all these predecessors, he ought to have ended it in a way to suggest that good ultimately triumphs over evil in this world and that, all in all, life makes sense. But that is clearly not what Shakespeare *felt*, and for that reason he chose instead to give it an ending that moved Dr. Johnson to write, "I was many years ago so shocked by Cordelia's death that I know not whether I ever endured to read again the last scenes of the play till I undertook to revise them as an editor," and that led Nahum Tate to restore the traditional happy ending in his revised version of the play, which, unbelievably, held the stage until 1838 because it was thought that, like Dr. Johnson, audiences would find the original simply more than they could stomach.

In addition to the ending, Shakespeare also changed the original by adding a subplot that he found in Sidney's *Arcadia*. Gloucester's story is in so many ways like Lear's—both old men are blindly mistaken about their children and suffer tragic consequence—that one wonders what it was that led Shakespeare to feel that he needed to say everything twice. Possibly he did it in order to show Lear as all the more towering a figure by contrasting him with Everyman. Proud, passionate, despotic, and generally wrongheaded, Lear nonetheless shouts down the hurricanoes that assail him and in the long run, although at unspeakable cost, becomes "every inch a king," whereas Gloucester, on the other hand—philandering, superstitious, gullible—is driven to escape his pain by attempting suicide in a scene so dangerously close to farce that Shakespeare must have known he was courting disaster as he wrote it. But by adding Gloucester to the play Shakespeare also seems to be saying that Lear's tragedy is no isolated instance of a single life gone wrong, but that life itself has gone wrong, and Everyman with it, in much the way that Ernest Hemingway famously put it in *A Farewell to Arms*: "The world kills the very good and the very gentle and the very brave impartially. If you are none of these you can be sure it will kill you too but there will be no special hurry." Ironically, it is old Gloucester who for the wrong reasons comes closest to getting it right. "These late eclipses of the sun and moon portend no good to us," he tells Edmund, who doesn't believe a word of it. "Love cools, friendships fall off, brothers divide. . . . Machinations, hollowness, treachery, and all ruinous disorders follow us disquietly to our graves."

"As flies to wanton boys are we to th' gods. / They kill us for their sport," is the devastating image that Gloucester uses after his blinding at the hands of Cornwall and Regan, and it is entirely in keeping with this bleak assessment of things. Lear, on the other hand, when he realizes that Cordelia has risked her life in returning from France with her armies to save him, says, "Upon such sacrifices, my Cordelia, / The gods themselves throw incense," and the most fateful question the play asks is which of these two views comes closer to describing the world at it really is. Is the truth beyond all truths that the gods, if they exist at all, are sadists, so that all of us, the good and bad alike, end up as their victims? Or is it that in hallowing such sacrifices as Cordelia's they reveal their true nature as above all else loving, so that even at our darkest moments they are with us and for us?

"The gods are just, and of our pleasant vices / Make instruments to scourge us," Edgar says, ignoring the fact that, as the play makes abundantly clear, the innocent are scourged right along with the guilty. Lear, by way of contrast, makes no claim that life under the gods is just, but only that it is so precious that, even in prison, he and Cordelia can "Pray, and sing, and tell old tales, and laugh . . ." And he goes further even than that. When he calls out,

"Hear, Nature, hear!" in cursing Goneril's un*natural* and therefore un*moral* behavior, he is assuming that, no matter what storms of the spirit we may have to endure, Nature is on the side of good over evil and thus we live in an essentially moral universe. Edmund's view is of course directly the opposite. When all by himself with no one to hear him he says, "Thou, Nature, art my goddess; to thy law / My services are bound," he is thinking of Nature simply as the way things are and of its only law as the law of the jungle.

Gods or no gods. Life as a divine comedy or life as a black comedy. These are the alternatives that hover in the wings throughout this most profoundly religious of all Shakespeare's plays and that haunt this saddest of all his stories as they plainly haunted him. It is a sadness that touches the heart with particular poignance because it is so often close to a kind of heartbreaking, heartbroken laughter, as in the scene where Gloucester in his blindness is led to believe that he is climbing a hill and then throwing himself off one of the Dover cliffs—Shakespeare the actor can't have been unaware that a single titter from the audience would destroy everything—or when Lear runs around mad as a hatter with weeds and nettles in his hair or mistakes Gloucester for "Goneril with a white beard." And supremely, of course, it is embodied in the character of the Fool, another of Shakespeare's major innovations, who has much to do with the tragedy's unique depth and emotional power.

Even before his first appearance toward the end of Act 1, we know that he "is not altogether fool, my lord," as Kent says, because when Lear complains of his not having been around for a couple of days—Goneril has already begun to slight him and he needs somebody to take his mind off his troubles—one of the knights volunteers that "since my young lady's going into France, sir, the fool hath much pined away," and pining away is not in the average fool's repertoire. Lear's response is to say, "No more of that; I have noted it well," so that before we ever see them on the stage together, we know much of the complex bond between them. The Fool has been pining away for Cordelia because she has been banished and also, one comes to realize, for Lear because he is aware that Lear is secretly pining away for her too. Nor is Lear any less aware of what is going on inside the Fool. He has noted the Fool's sorrow well and cuts the knight off short because it is the only way he can deal with the whole sorrowful situation, which he is beginning to see he has brought down not just on the Fool, but on all of them through his folly. But the Fool will not let him get away with "No more of that." On the contrary, his whole purpose in staying with him and sharing his misery is to show him more and still more of who he is and of what he has done in his madness and folly, in the hope of somehow helping to save his soul even if it means breaking his heart in the process, not to mention breaking his own heart as well. As soon as he enters, he starts trying to face him with the truth about himself through riddles and jingles because he knows that Lear is too proud and too stubborn to listen to it in any other form. When he hands Lear his coxcomb for "having banish'd two on's daughters, and [done] the third a blessing against his will," Lear responds with "Take heed, sirrah—the whip," but it is hard to take him seriously, because he so clearly treasures and needs the Fool quite as much as the Fool treasures and needs him. The relationship between them is as moving and convincing as any other in the play.

I picture the Fool not as in whiteface—fragile, androgynous, harlequinesque—but rather as like some old vaudevillian who no longer gets the laughs he once did and is close enough to Lear's age to know what it's like to feel over the hill and superfluous. The snatches of half-remembered songs that he rattles off, the gags, the ribaldries don't even seem to amuse himself much anymore, let alone anybody else, but he keeps them coming through thick and thin anyway. Sometimes they serve the purpose simply of trying to cheer the old man up as when, with a bump and grind, he exits on "She that's a maid now, and laughs at my departure, / Shall not be a maid long, unless things be cut shorter," but at other times they draw blood. "Fathers that wear rags / Shall see their children blind; / But fathers that bear bags / Shall see their children kind," he says, and terrible truth of it makes Lear suddenly afraid that he is going mad—"O, how this mother swells towards my heart! / Hysterica passio! Thou climbing sorrow! / Thy element's below."

By basing his play on a chapter from Britain's remote, pre-Christian past, Shakespeare prudently avoided a direct confrontation with the church of his day and also steered clear of any explicit allusion to Christian beliefs, but, as you might expect, it is the endlessly imprudent Fool who in another of his sallies all but comes out with one of them:

> That sir which serves and seeks for gain,
> And follows but for form,
> Will pack when it begins to rain

And leave thee in the storm.
But I will tarry; the fool will stay,
And let the wise man fly.
The knave turns fool that runs away;
The fool no knave, perdy.

Only a fool, in other words, would stay with a man who is down on his luck when the wise thing is clearly to abandon him before being sucked down into his bad luck with him, and yet in the long run the ones who abandon him are not only knaves in so doing, but also fools in the sense that they do not see that they are dehumanizing themselves in the process. The fool who stays with him, on the other hand, is—to put it negatively—"no knave, perdy," with "perdy" as a corrupt form of "par Dieu," which marks the closest Shakespeare comes to saying in so many words, perhaps even to believing, that in sacrificing himself for his friend, the Fool becomes God's fool or, in Paul's phrase, a fool for Christ's sake.

It is in First Corinthians that Paul also writes, "God chose what is foolish in the world to shame the wise, God chose what is weak in the world to shame the strong, God chose what is low and despised in the world, even things that are not, to bring to nothing things that are," and the echoes of those words in *King Lear* are so striking that it is hard to believe that they were not consciously in Shakespeare's mind as he wrote it. Not only are the foolish wise in his play and the wise foolish, just as the weak are strong in it and the strong weak, but what seems to be *nothing*—a word that Lear and Cordelia, Edmund and Gloucester, and the Fool all play upon at some length—turns out to be something of surpassing importance, as it does when in answer to Lear's "What can you say to draw a third more opulent than your sisters?" Cordelia's "nothing" contains the whole richness and truth of her love contrasted with her sister's deceit. It is almost possible to think of Shakespeare as having written the entire play as a gloss on St. Paul, adding to it such other paradoxes of his own, as that it is the sane who are mad and the mad sane, just as it is also the blind who see and the seeing who are blind.

The "wise" characters are of course Goneril, Regan, Cornwall, and Edmund, and what they are wise to is how to achieve their own ends at no matter what cost, as when Goneril and Regan dupe their father into dividing his kingdom between them and when Edmund convinces Gloucester that Edgar is a scoundrel in order to establish himself as heir apparent in his place. What they never fail to see in their wisdom is which way the wind is blowing so that they can chart their courses accordingly, but when Albany, appalled by Goneril's mistreatment of her father, says, "How far your eyes may pierce I cannot tell," it raises the question as to what not only she but all of the wise ones fail to see entirely, cunning though they are. The scene in which that question is first answered through dramatic action marks what is in a sense the turning point of the play.

There are two trials in the third act. In the first of them, which takes place in the hovel where he has taken shelter from the storm, Lear in his madness imagines that Goneril is being tried for having "kicked the poor king her father," as he puts it, and appoints Edgar, disguised as Poor Tom the Bedlam beggar, and the Fool to stand as justicers. It is all sheer lunacy, of course, but in view of the fact that Goneril, although present only in Lear's mind, is unquestionably guilty as charged and that, appearances to the contrary notwith-standing, Edgar and the Fool are eminently qualified by their integrity to judge her, it is a model of sanity when compared to the one that immediately follows it.

In the second trial, Gloucester is hauled in before a kangaroo court consisting of Regan and Cornwall, who, having learned through Edmund that the old man has taken pity on Lear in his suffering, charge him with being "a filthy traitor" and assail him with questions and accusations that fly so fast he scarcely has time to answer them. They vilify him. Regan wrenches hair from his beard. There is not even the pretense of justice. And then in a scene that even on the printed page makes the blood run cold, Cornwall, egged on by Regan, has him pinioned to his chair and with his own hands gouges out one of his eyes. Up to this point, it is the strong ones who have prevailed over the weak, the wise ones over the foolish, but then, suddenly and unforeseeably, the tide turns. Just as Cornwall is about to gouge out Gloucester's second eye, one of the unnamed servants is so revolted by what is going on that when he fails in his attempt to stop it, he draws a sword and kills Cornwall, only then to be killed himself by Regan, who comes up from behind and stabs him.

Piercing as the eyes of Cornwall and Regan are and wise as they are to the ways of others as ruthless and duplicitous as themselves, what they are completely blind to is that, in addition to ruthless-ness and duplicity, there also dwells in the human heart an essen-tial humanness by disregarding which—not only in the unnamed servant but also in themselves—they bring about their own down-fall. And the same is true also of Edmund.

Playing with the affections of Goneril and Regan solely for the purpose of realizing his own imperial ambitions, Edmund never for a moment suspects that for them it is not a game at all because, though he has never guessed it, they have so helplessly lost their hearts to him that each of them is prepared to kill or be killed in the effort to make him her own. He was always fully aware that they were as unscrupulous and conniving as he was, but it is only when he looks down at their dead faces in the final scene of the play that he becomes aware of this other dimension of them as well, and it is with a kind of dazed incredulity that with his dying breath he says, "Yet Edmund was belov'd. / The one the other poisoned for my sake, / And after slew herself," thunderstruck as much by what he has found out about himself as by what he has found out about them. If anything can explain his sudden change of heart in attempting at the last moment to save the lives of Lear and Cordelia, whom he had ordered slain, it is that here at the end he discovers for the first time that he has a heart to change.

When Kent, following Lear's banishment of himself as well as Cordelia, says, "See better, Lear," he could as well be talking to virtually any character in the play. The good ones and the evil ones alike, what do they see and what do they fail to see? What in particular does Lear fail to see when he first gathers his court about him to witness the ceremonial passing on of power to his daughters, and what does he gradually come to see better and better until it drives him mad and all but destroys him? In the dark world of the play—a great deal of which takes place in literal darkness—what hope is there that somewhere there is light? And how about the world itself, including Shakespeare's world, where fathers like his own fall from honor to dishonor, where childeren like his own die in childhood, where friends betray friends and lovers lovers.

From the very first scene of the play, where Lear swears by "the sacred radiance of the sun, / The mysteries of Hecate and the night," to the very last where he says, "Mine eyes are not o' th' best" and Albany brings the play to an end with "The oldest have borne most; we that are young / Shall never *see* so much, nor live so long," the play so abounds with images of light and dark, sight and blindness, that we are never for a moment allowed to forget this major theme; and for those who might miss it even so, it is of course physically acted out on the stage. It is when Gloucester is blinded that he at last sees the truth about his two sons and says, "I stumbled when I saw," meaning that it is not with the eyes of his head that he has seen it, but with the eyes of his heart—another kind of seeing, another kind of light.

The reason that Lear does not see that Goneril and Regan are duping him is that he does not want to see it, and the reason he does not see that Cordelia is the one who really loves him is that she so hurts his pride by not being willing to dissimulate like her sisters that he angrily refuses to see it. He does not see that Kent is right in accusing him of "hideous rashness" because once again his pride as well as his honor keep him from seeing it, and he does not see what it is that with his songs and sad jokes the Fool is constantly trying to tell him because what the Fool is constantly trying to tell him above all else is the truth about himself, the sight of which he is afraid will turn him to stone. He is so absorbed in his own sorrows and regrets that he does not see that the Fool is not just a diverting foil to have around in a crisis, but also a human being like himself, and it is only when he realizes that the Fool's teeth are chattering like his own as they stand together there in the wind and pelting rain that he finds it in him to say at last, to see at last, "Poor fool and knave, I have one part in my heart / That's sorry yet for thee." From there it is a relatively short step to seeing farther still into a whole world of suffering, and out of this deepened vision comes the unforgettable prayer that he addresses not to the gods, as he does elsewhere, but to the people he is praying for—and also, in a sense, to himself:

> *Poor, naked wretches, wheresoe'er you are,*
> *That bide the pelting of this pitiless storm,*
> *How shall your houseless heads and unfed sides,*
> *Your loop'd and window'd raggedness, defend you*
> *From seasons such as these? O, I have ta'en*
> *Too little care of this! Take physic, pomp;*
> *Expose thyself to feel what wretches feel,*
> *That thou mayst shake the superflux to them*
> *And show the heavens more just.*

By saying "To show the heavens more just," Lear means that because the heavens, if they exist at all in the sense of divine providence, seem to be as indifferent to the naked wretches of the world as he himself always was, there are none to do them justice, if it is to be done at all, except for people like him who have the means for doing it. This is farther than he has ever seen before, and it opens up that one part of his heart that is sorry for the Fool to include multitudes.

It is only at the end of the play that he comes to see farther even than that. It is the last time that Shakespeare shows him and Cordelia together. The British forces have defeated the invading French, Edmund has ordered the pair of them to be taken away under guard, and what Lear says as they wait to go gives a sense less of words written for effect by a great dramatist than of words the dramatist was great enough to be able to step back and leave the old king free to speak as if out of his own truth.

> *Come, let's away to prison.*
> *We two alone will sing like birds i' th' cage.*
> *When thou dost ask me blessing, I'll kneel down*
> *And ask of thee forgiveness. So we'll live,*
> *And pray, and sing, and tell old tales, and laugh*
> *At gilded butterflies, and hear poor rogues*
> *Talk of court news; and we'll talk with them too—*
> *Who loses and who wins; who's in, who's out—*
> *And take upon 's the mystery of things,*
> *As if we were God's spies; and we'll wear out,*
> *In a wall'd prison, packs and sects of great ones*
> *That ebb and flow by th' moon.*

"See better, Lear," Kent admonished him in the first act, and here in the last he sees into the mystery that lies beyond both tragedy and comedy with something that approaches the Olympian detachment, the transcendent serenity, not of "the gods" this time, but of God himself. There is nothing high-flown about what he says. His language could hardly be plainer or less adorned, his meaning more clear. It is not a tragic hero speaking blank verse that we are given here, but simply an old man speaking as he might in life itself. It was out of his own deepest humanity that Shakespeare dreamed these lines, and few he ever wrote are as moving or ring as true.

In *Huckleberry Finn* virtually everybody lies, the innocent like Huck and Jim in order to survive in a hostile world and the corrupt like the Duke and the Dauphin in order to take advantage of the innocent. In *King Lear,* much the same is true. First and foremost, of course, Goneril and Regan lie to their father, but they are mere amateurs compared to Edmund, who lies to his father about being the dutiful son protecting him against the villainous Edgar, to Edgar about being the faithful brother protecting him against their father's wrath, to Regan and Cornwall about being one "Whose virtue and obedience doth this instant / So much commend itself," as Cornwall tells him, that he is accepted by them as their most trusted friend, and to both Goneril and Regan with the result that each comes to believe that it is she rather than her sister who has caught his fancy. Edmund, in fact, lies on such a heroic scale that he himself would appear to be the only one in the play to know who he truly is if it were not that he fails until almost the end of his life to realize that, scoundrel though he recognizes himself to be, there is something in him that Goneril and Regan did not just lust for, but actually loved enough to kill for. He was blind, in other words, to something human and capable of stirring love that was buried so deep within him that it had somehow survived all that he had done to destroy it, and in this he resembles Lear.

The world that drives Lear mad is a world where not only do

evil ones like Goneril, Regan, and Edmund lie in order to dupe the unwary, but a good one like Kent is obliged to lie in the sense of disguising himself as Caius, the plain-spoken servant, because Lear has banished him under pain of death for having tried to save him by telling him the plain truth. No one loves Lear better than Kent does, but such is the madness not only of Lear, but of the whole world of the play that he does not dare show it openly and honestly any more than the Fool dares show his love of Lear by confronting him with his folly openly and honestly. It is only at the end that, like Edmund, Lear sees for the first time that in spite of all the darkness within him there is also, though he never guessed it, something that others find precious enough to give their lives for.

When the Doctor and Cordelia wake him with music after his ordeal on the heath, it is at first only the darkness that he can see. "I am bound / Upon a wheel of fire, that mine own tears / Do scald like molten lead," are the words he calls it by, and when Cordelia tries to kneel for him to bless her, he tells her not to mock him because he cannot believe that she can find anything in him worth kneeling to. "I am a very foolish fond old man," he says, because he has come to know that about himself as well, and "I fear I am not in my right mind," as he gradually comes awake and tries to make out where he is and who these people are that he finds with him. Once he realizes that the young woman in tears at his side is his daughter Cordelia, he says, "I know you do not love me; for your sisters / Have, as I do remember, done me wrong. / You have some cause, they have not," and it is only when in one of the most moving moments in the play she says simply, "No cause.

No cause," that he can believe at last that she not only loves him, but loves him enough to have come back from France at the risk of her life to save him. Nor is there any doubt in his mind as to the nature of that love. "Upon such sacrifices, my Cordelia," he says as they await being led away to prison, "The gods themselves throw incense."

What is Shakespeare saying in all this about the weight of time's sadness? He seems to be saying that more often than not people are blind not only to each other, including the poor naked wretches of the world, but also to themselves, the best as well as the worst, and that King Lear is far from being the only one who, in Regan's cutting words to him, "hath ever but slenderly known himself." The ones who come closest to knowing themselves, to knowing at least their own hearts, are Kent and the Fool, but such is the blindness of the ones they have given their hearts to that they can be faithful to them only in secret. In the opening scene Cordelia could so easily have prevented the whole tragic sequence of events simply by telling her father that she loved him, which was both what he wanted to hear and also the truth, but instead—out of a stubbornness not unlike his own, perhaps, or out of the impulse to expose her sisters for the hypocrites she knew them to be—she chose instead to "Love, and be silent," revealing the truth to him only when it was too late. None of them in the play, neither the good nor the evil, are entirely what they seem.

Nor is it by any means only love that hides its face. Lear especially is the one who inveighs against humans for hiding the beast in themselves. He speaks of his "pelican daughters" who feed on his bleeding flesh, and assails one or the other of them as variously "detested kite," "wolvish," "vulture," "serpent." Albany calls them "tigers, not daughters," and says "even the head-lugged" bear would have behaved more humanely than they to their father. Never guessing that he is planting the seeds of his own mutilation in their minds, Gloucester tells Regan that he has sent Lear to Dover because "I would not see thy cruel nails / Pluck out his poor old eyes; nor thy fierce sister / In his anointed flesh stick boarish fangs," and "If that the heavens do not their visible spirits / Send quickly down to tame these vile offenses," Albany says, "It will come, / Humanity must perforce prey on itself, / Like monsters of the deep." Even the virtuous Edgar describes himself as monstrous—"hog in sloth, fox in stealth, wolf in greediness, dog in madness, lion in prey."

What Lear is obsessed by in human beings, however, is not so much the beast in them in general as what he sees to be their ravening sexuality in particular, and since there is nothing in the plot that seems to explain why this should so preoccupy him, it seems not unreasonable to suppose that the preoccupation was to some degree, and for reasons one can only guess at, Shakespeare's, especially considering that he seems to be similarly preoccupied in such other plays of roughly this same period in his life as *Othello*, *Measure for Measure*, and *Hamlet*, although in none of them so extensively and so passionately. When Lear calls upon the raging elements to do their worst until they have "drench'd our steeples, drown'd the cocks," bidding the thunder to "strike flat the thick rotundity of the world, / Crack Nature's moulds, all germains spill at once, / That make ungrateful man," all those images of tumescence make it clear enough what it is about man's animal nature that most horrifies him, and elsewhere in his ravings he addresses it explicitly. "Thou rascal beadle, hold thy bloody hand!" he cries out in one of his hallucinations. "Why dost thou lash that whore? Strip thine own back. / Thou hotly lusts to use her in that kind / For which thou whip'st her," and he is equally scathing in his picture of "yond simp'ring dame, / Whose face between her forks presageth snow, / That minces virtue, and does shake the head / To hear of pleasure's name" whereas not even "the fitchew nor the soiled horse goes to 't / With a more riotous appetite," adding that "Down from the waist they are Centaurs, / Though women all above. / But to the girdle do the gods inherit, / Beneath is all the fiend's," and then lapsing into an explosion of sexual nausea that borders on incoherence with "There's hell, there's darkness, there's the sulphurous pit; / Burning, scalding, stench, consumption. Fie, fie, fie! / pah, pah!" In *The Man Who Was Thursday*, the terrifying disguises are removed one by one to reveal the human reality beneath. As Lear sees it, exactly the reverse is true.

The play is as rich in clothes images as it is in images of animals, of sight and blindness, of light and dark, all of them recurring again and again throughout the text with the effect of giving the same sense of life and movement to the play's major themes as pictures of a man in various stages of riding a horse, say, give the sense of life and movement when you riffle through them with your thumb. Clothes signify disguise either literally, as in the case of Kent and Edgar, or figuratively, as in Cordelia's saying to her sisters, "Time shall unfold what plighted [in the sense of *plaited* or *enfolded*] cunning hides. / Who covers faults, at last shame them derides." Clothes also represent the burden of kingship that Lear "divests" himself of in the opening scene, or power like the "many folds of favor" that Cordelia "dismantles" by refusing to tell her father what he wants to hear, and so on. But perhaps most importantly of all, clothes represent defense against what the play portrays as a world full of darkness and threat.

"Be not afeard: the isle is full of noises, / Sounds and sweet airs that give delight and hurt not," Caliban says in what is possibly the last of the plays, *The Tempest*, a fairy tale too good not to be true, where all shadows are finally dispelled and the world seems bathed in a kind of golden haze, as if at the close of his career Shakespeare had reached some kind of golden inner peace within himself. But not so *King Lear*. "Thou know'st, the first time that we smell the air / We wawl and cry," Lear says, "cry that we are come / To this great stage of fools," cry because the air is so far from sweet and unhurtful that the first time we breathe it we know we are doomed. Life is full not of sounds and sweet airs, but is a storm as pitiless as the one that the poor in their "loop'd and window'd raggedness" are defenseless against and that Lear and the Fool seek shelter from on the heath. Nor is it just the innocent who are vulnerable to its raging. Regan tries to protect herself against it with the accoutrements of power, represented, as Lear tells her, by what "thou gorgeous wear'st / Which scarcely keeps thee warm," and it is not just old Gloucester, one senses, that Cornwall hates with such savagery, but the whole stormy world that he feels betrayed and threatened by, and it is because Edmund sees the world as having no law apart from the law of the jungle that he connives with the ruthlessness and stealth of a jackal to keep the other predators at bay. Ultimately they all of them, the good and the bad alike, prove defenseless against the hostility of the world, but what Shakespeare seems to be saying as he weighs the sadness of it is that Edgar in the rags of a Bedlam beggar, the Fool soaked to the skin in his motley, Gloucester in his blindness, and Kent and Cordelia in their banishment are all somehow ennobled by their battle with it even though it ends in defeat. When Lear looks at Edgar in his near nakedness, he says, "Thou art the thing itself; unaccommodated man is no more but such a poor, bare, forked animal as thou art," but if human beings are no more than that, they are also no less the way Goneril and Regan in their rapacity are less by being subhuman, subanimal. The words are no sooner out of Lear's mouth than he starts trying to tear off his own clothes, as if in his mantic frenzy he sees that in the proud regalia of kingship his life was, impoverished and dehumanized whereas crowned only with weeds and nettles and robed in tatters he has become "every inch a king."

It is the naked victims of the world, in other words, who survive in spirit, and one thinks again of Hopkins' "passing stranger" transfigured by swimming naked in the river, of the nakedness of Huck and Jim drifting toward freedom on their raft, and of Gabriel Syme exchanging the grey suit he masqueraded in as an anarchist for the blue and gold robe of the Fourth Day of Creation. "God chose what is weak in the world to shame the strong," is the way St. Paul put it, and it is perhaps the central paradox of the play.

The first *King Lear* I ever attended was an amateur production at Princeton University either during my senior year there or shortly afterwards. The Théatre Intime, where it was given, held only about seventy-five seats or so, I think, and the stage was very small. The part of Lear was played by an undergraduate named Moe Kinnan, who like the rest of the cast can't have been much more than twenty or so, the sets were minimal, the stagecraft amateurish, and yet no production I have seen since has moved me so deeply. I have never forgotten that boy making his final entrance as Lear with Cordelia's dead body in his arms, and I can still remember the stunning impact of his "Howl, howl, howl, howl!" It is not hard to understand why for years Dr. Johnson was unable to read that scene again or why even after countless readings it remains so devastating.

Lear refuses to believe that his daughter is dead and when he doesn't hear her speak thinks that maybe it is only because "Her voice was ever soft, / Gentle, and low—an excellent thing in woman" and that perhaps his hearing has failed him. He has an old man's pride at having had strength enough to kill the man who hanged her and remembers how there once was a time when "with my good biting falchion / I would have made them skip." He is not sure who Kent is. He scarcely registers the news of his older daughters' deaths and makes no response at all when a captain comes in with word that Edmund has been slain by Edgar in trial by combat. Even when Albany announces that he will be given back the throne for the rest of his days, it is as if Lear hasn't so much as heard him.

"My poor fool is hang'd!" he says in the sense of "my poor innocent, my poor darling," but also in the sense of "But I will tarry; the fool will stay," which the Fool himself stayed and sang to him in the rain. Then,

"No, no, no life!
Why should a dog, a horse, a rat, have life,
And thou no breath at all? Thou'lt come no more,
Never, never, never, never, never!"

By saying "never" five times as he said "no" three and "howl" four, the words become bearers less of meaning now than simply of all that is meaningless and unbearable.

Then, "Pray you, undo this button," and "Thank you, sir," as, perhaps only in his imagination, someone helps him to undo it. It is the ultimate divesting of himself, the final exposure of himself to feel what wretches feel, a last echo of "Off, off, you lendings!" as on the heath he tried to tear off everything that stood between him and "the thing itself."

"Do you see this? Look on her! look! Her lips! / Look there, look there!" are the last of his words as he dies believing she lives because it is beyond him to believe anything else, and who knows? Is it possible that we are being asked to wonder if, as one of God's spies, he saw deeper into the mystery of things than any of them?

By the time the curtain falls the evil ones have all died and most of the good ones too. Edgar tells us that Gloucester's "flaw'd heart ... 'twixt two extremes of passion, joy and grief, / Burst smilingly," and the Fool, his sad work done, has long since vanished. When someone tries to stir Lear to life, Kent says, "He hates him / That would upon the rack of this tough world / Stretch him out longer," and hints that he himself will soon be following him. But it is of course Cordelia's death—within seconds of the rescue that would have given the play the same happy ending that all other versions of the old tale had given it—that for more than two hundred years kept it from being presented as Shakespeare wrote it. It was simply too dark for audiences to endure.

At the end, the stage is so littered with corpses that there is almost no one left except Albany, with all the "milky gentleness" that Goneril accused him of, to stammer the curtain down as best he can with his

The weight of this sad time we must obey,
Speak what we feel, not what we ought to say.

What Shakespeare asks of his audience is a suspension not only of disbelief—and belief along with it—but of the inclination to view life as either tragic or comic, or as sometimes one and sometimes the other. Life is continually both at once is what his obedience to time's sadness led him to say, and what he *felt* about it and opened his veins to make his audience feel along with him was that it was precisely that quality that constituted the richness of it, and the terror of it, and the heartbreaking beauty of it, which perhaps it took a man facing old age and death, as Shakespeare himself was on the brink of facing them, to see. It is also to be noted that in every scene of great suffering, he has someone enter from the wings to relieve it.

Life is tragicomic at best, he seems to be saying, but if people like Cordelia, the Fool, Edgar, and Kent keep being born into it, and if Lear is right about what the gods hallow, then perhaps not quite everything is lost. The opening scene of the play has a fairy-tale quality about it, with the two wicked sisters and the one good one, as in Cinderella, and the richest treasure going to the one who gives the best speech as to the one who makes the right wish or opens the right casket, but it isn't long before Shakespeare turns all this on its head and the hope that they will all live happily ever after gets lost in nightmare. And yet, and yet, he seems to say, maybe life is like a fairy tale notwithstanding, if only in the sense that all disguises are stripped away in the end and all evil spells undone, so that even the Beast becomes beautiful when he discovers that Beauty loves him, and even the old king, with Beauty dead in his arms, finally becomes a human being, and the last word, like Albany's, is a word of mercy.

AFTERWORD

You picture them, one by one, as they sit down to their work. The despondent little Jesuit drudge in his rusty black clericals and gaping dog collar. Maybe he is in the university library, with its shelves still mostly empty from the bishop's pillaging, or in his small third-floor room in Newman House looking down on gray Dublin. His tea has gone cold at his elbow. His eyes are red-rimmed and watery from the endless papers. He has laid his pencil down and is watching the movement of a raindrop on the window-pane as it zigzags its way in fits and starts until it meets another, hesitates for an instant, merges, and is lost.

Mark Twain is in his octagonal study in Elmira, New York, with its hilltop view of the Chemung River. The air is blue with pipe smoke. He is still in his forties, and his hair hasn't turned snowy yet. He has kicked off his shoes and is wearing the pantoufles that Joe Twichell bought him in Paris once. It is getting on toward the end of a summer afternoon and soon he will amble down to the main house to join Livy and the girls, but for the moment he is aware only of the power of the great current that carries him along like a raft.

Who can possibly guess where Chesterton is? In a tea room with a cigarette between his lips and one eye squinted against the smoke? On the upper deck of a bus, his pince-nez glittering in the sun? In Kensington Gardens with his slouch hat on the bench beside him and, wrapped up in it, a buttered scone? He is so massive in his flowing cape that his penny exercise book looks more like a penny stamp, or maybe he is writing on the back of his program during an intermission at Covent Garden. In the margin he has inked in two or three goblin faces on a curlicue vine.

The domed forehead, the owlish gaze, the skimpy whiskers—did the man who wrote the plays look anything at all like the Droeshout engraving that adorns their first collected edition? Can we even be entirely sure that he was Will Shakespeare, the improvident glover's son, or is it just barely possible that, all arguments to the contrary notwithstanding, he actually was the Earl of Oxford or Sir Francis Bacon or heaven knows which of the others who have been put forward over the years? Even the ordinary sounds and smells and sights of his time can only be guessed at—the way the English language sounded when Gloriana spoke it, the way the city of London looked before it burned down, the cries from the streets, the quality of darkness when there were nothing but flames to light it, the very scent of the air before the Industrial Revolution changed it forever. All we can be sure of is that he had a pen in his hand, a mind to move it, and a heart weighed down by whatever the saddest things were that had ever happened to him, which, like the Duke of Albany, he felt he could honor best by opening a vein and writing about them not as he ought, but as a tale of treachery and self-sacrifice, of love and lust, of madness and blindness, of wisdom and folly, in a world where nothing is entirely what it seems. Never before and never afterwards did he write anything with such extraordinary care—the intricately recurring images, the fuguelike themes, the meanings within meaning. To what extent and in what ways it was also the tale of his own life is left for us to guess at along with his sexual tastes and the identity of the Dark Lady.

To think of these four superstars as having come somehow to terms with the weight of their sad times in writing these four very different works is to ask myself to what extent, in a minor role, I have done something of the same in writing this one. Over the last fifty years or so I have both directly in my various memoirs and indirectly in my novels tried to deal with as best I could—to understand as fully, to lay to rest as finally—the dark shadow that my father's suicide continues to cast over my days even now that more than sixty-five years have passed since it occurred in my childhood. But this book I thought of as a kind of vacation from all that—a chance to shift my gaze from inward to outward, to the shadowy side of lives other than mine. And so it turned out to be, but with an added reward that I did not see coming. It was a matter not just of listening to other people's voices for a change instead of to my own, but of hearing those voices speak more relevantly and healingly to my condition than I foresaw.

Like anyone else pushing seventy-five, the stage I hold forth on, like Albany's, is littered with the dead, including my only brother, my oldest friend, and an increasing number of others I always assumed would be with me till the final curtain rings down. In addition to that, my body is no longer altogether the one I have depended on and enjoyed and neglected all these years, with the result that all sorts of things I thought I would be able to go on doing more or less indefinitely are slipping out of reach and I am still young enough in my mind to bridle at it.

Death, on the other hand, seems less of a negative to me now than it once did. If somebody a while back had offered me a thousand more years, I would have leapt at it, but at this point I would be inclined to beg off on the grounds that, although I continue to enjoy things a good deal most of the time and hope to go on as long as I can, the eventual end to life seems preferable to the idea of an endless and endlessly redundant extension of it. The only really sad part of checking out as I think of it now is that I won't be around to see what becomes of my grandchildren, who are the light of my life, the oldest of them only seven at this writing. But maybe that is just as well. They say that we are never happier than our unhappiest child, and if that is expanded to include the next generation down, the result is unthinkable.

There is sadness too in thinking how much more I might have done with my life than just writing, especially considering that I was ordained not only to preach good news to the poor, but to feed the hungry, clothe the naked, visit the sick and the imprisoned, and raise the dead. If I make it as far as St. Peter's gate, the most I will be able to plead is my thirty-two books, and if that is not enough, I am lost. My faith has never been threatened as agonizingly as Chesterton's or Hopkins', or simply abandoned like Mark Twain's, or held in such perilous tension with unfaith as Shakespeare's. I have never looked into the abyss, for which I am thankful. But I wish such faith as I have had been brighter and gladder. I wish I had done more with it. I wish I had been braver and bolder. I wish I had been a saint.

This, in short, is the weight of my own sad times, and listening to these four voices speaking out from under the burden of theirs has been to find not just a kind of temporary release, but a kind of unexpected encouragement.

Take heart, I heard them say, even at the unlikeliest moments. Fear not. Be alive. Be merciful. Be human. And most unlikely of all: Even when you can't believe, even if you don't believe at all, even if you shy away at the sound of his name, be Christ.